Rachel —
Praying God's
best blessings
for you & your
family.
Deanna
Rokke

Winning Women Pray

BEFORE, DURING, & AFTER

CATHY MESSECAR
& DEANNA KOEHL

LEAFWOOD
PUBLISHERS
an imprint of Abilene Christian University Press

WINNING WOMEN PRAY
Before, During, and After

LEAFWOOD

P U B L I S H E R S

an imprint of Abilene Christian University Press

Copyright © 2017 by Cathy Messecar and Deanna Koehl

ISBN 978-0-89112-472-6 | LCCN 2017001788

Printed in the United States of America

LIBRARY OF CONGRESS CATALOGING-IN-PUBLICATION DATA
Names: Messecar, Cathy, author.
Title: Winning women pray : before, during, and after / Cathy Messecar and
    Deanna Koehl.
Description: Abilene, Texas : Leafwood Publishers, 2017.
Identifiers: LCCN 2017001788 | ISBN 9780891124726 (pbk.)
Subjects: LCSH: Christian women—Religious life. | Prayer—Christianity. |
    Prayer—Biblical teaching.
Classification: LCC BV4527 .M4378 2017 | DDC 248.3/2082—dc23
LC record available at https://lccn.loc.gov/ 2017001788

Cover design by ThinkPen Design, LLC
Interior text design by Sandy Armstrong, Strong Design

Leafwood Publishers is an imprint of Abilene Christian University Press
ACU Box 29138
Abilene, Texas 79699

1-877-816-4455
www.leafwoodpublishers.com

17 18 19 20 21 22 / 7 6 5 4 3 2 1

To my Cowboy,
who prays for me from the saddle.
—Deanna

To my daughter, Sheryle Bazan,
who encourages me through texted prayers.
—Cathy

Acknowledgments

We send sincere thanks to . . .

the women's Bible class who first heard this material in the raw,

our early readers: Russell Stewart, Doris Allen, and Sherry Rushing,

our families, who cheer and encourage our writing and teaching,

the staff at Leafwood Publishers, especially our editor, Mary Hardegree,

to all who have taught us the discipline of prayer,

to Jesus, who continues to intercede for all believers.

During the days of Jesus' life on earth, he offered up prayers and petitions with fervent cries and tears to the one who could save him from death, and he was heard because of his reverent submission.

—Hebrews 5:7 <small>NIV</small>

Contents

After Prayers

Dear Winning Woman,

"Prayer warrior" describes a person of fervent prayer, the phrase bandied among Christians. Yet how many women rely on personal planning first, instead of entreating God? Who among us battles in prayer for the salvation of the world—that God's will be done on earth as in heaven? Do intercessory prayers rise each day or many "me, me, me" prayers? When asked to pray for another's job search, health, or salvation, and we answer that we will, how many of us keep that prayer promise?

How can we develop the habit of covering our families and communities in prayer *before* needs arise? How do our passionate prayers *during* a crisis affect God? Do we remember to give thanks *after* storms have passed?

We don't have all the answers, but when we shared this series with women in our home congregation, we found many instances of biblical prayers that were prayed *before*, *during*, and *after*. Immediately after embarking on this study, we found ourselves saying to the Lord: "This is a *before* prayer. I'm asking for this child to grow in your grace." "I'm in the middle of a crisis.

I need your wisdom." "Father, how good you are. You saw my need before I asked. Thank you."

Jesus prayed before his ministry began, during, and after. As our high priest, he continues to intercede for us at the right hand of God. King David prayed before battles, during trials, and after repentance. Elijah prayed before rain fell. Moses prayed during crises. Eve declared in praise that God's help got her through the pain of that first childbirth.

Winning Women Pray will follow the format of our previous book (*Winning Every Woman's War: Defeating Temptations*). You will find examples of prayer from Jesus and personal stories from Deanna and Cathy (**In the Trenches**). In this series, *Sword, Shield, and Shoes,* we encourage you to personalize the Word of God, your **Sword**; we cheer you toward a greater **Shield** of faith; and we applaud your **Shoes** of readiness, willing to pray "in every circumstance."

The **Historical Field Guide** will offer contemporary and past vignettes about prayer. Just as a soldier's dog tag reminds the wearer of his or her vulnerability, **My Dog Tag Bible** verses remind you of God's constant help and nearness as you battle against evil through prayer.

Each chapter ends with **Tactical Training**, eight questions that allow you to read Scriptures, reflect, and write conclusions. We challenge you to expect God's nonstop presence in your life and record in **My Diary from the Trenches** how God blesses as he battles alongside you, teaching you to pray. You will pray **My Combat Prayer** each day of the twelve-week study, and by the end, you will have settled into better prayer habits. We want you to practice prayer, not just study about prayer.

A wife, mother, and grandmother, Cathy Messecar lives in the trenches of the sandwich generation, while Deanna Koehl—a wife and mother—remains stationed in homeschooling and chauffeuring. We both assist in our home-based family businesses. We joined ranks to write a book that represents both arenas of Titus 2, the older woman and the younger woman. We have prayed that you will gain a new awareness of God's armor, presence, holiness, and help.

Grab your pen and Bible, do the written work, do the prayer work, and watch as God works in you.

In the trenches with you,
Cathy Messecar and Deanna Koehl

Chapter One

Pray—Before, During, and After

"Pray without ceasing." —1 Thessalonians 5:17

Prayer—possibly the most discussed topic in Christendom and the least practiced.

Jesus said prayer can move mountains; however, most people simply *use* prayer for clearing unwanted dust from their personal lives. Why don't we take prayer more seriously? Why is prayer so often the last resort in a mess? Unfortunately, most replies are drenched in pride. Why pray if we can handle life on our own? Self-made and pulled up by our own designer boot-straps, prayer time seems pointless—just another activity on an already full schedule.

But what if . . . prayer really is all God says it is? What if reaching God through prayer could revive a family? What if communicating with our Father could change the course of a city, a country, or the world? What if the promised power infused our lives, changed our hearts, and healed old wounds? Would we pray if we truly believed in the promised blessings? When would we pray and how would we pray, if we embraced God's truth about prayer?

We *would* "pray without ceasing." We *would* pray *before*, *during*, and *after*.

The pages of the Bible abound with stories of men and women who prayed *before* an event, *during* the chaos of life, and *after* lives settled. Those prayers prepared, equipped, praised, and cast out fears. Prayer wasn't something the biblical heroes did for God. God gifted them with the communication of prayer because prayer connects us to God, and that connection changes our hearts, often our circumstances, and always our lives. We can't afford to forfeit all God has for us by neglecting the gift of prayer.

Jesus's Prayer Life Investigated

When the prayer life of Jesus falls under a microscope, an abundance of evidence supports the necessity of prayer *before*, *during*, and *after*. He prayed before he began his earthly ministry. Immediately after his baptism, the Spirit led him into the wilderness for a time of prayer and fasting. The enemy intruded on this time with intense temptations but failed to gain Jesus's allegiance. Jesus prayed in the garden before his betrayal and crucifixion. This time of prayer, while short, was passionate. These constant before prayers equipped him for the trials and opportunities that lay ahead. Jesus prayed *before*.

He cried out during the storm on the sea, bringing calm for the waves and his disciples. He prayed during his time on the cross. While hanging in pain, he sought comfort and strength from his Father. During prayers, often the most intense, bring troubled thoughts before God and remind us of who helps us. Jesus prayed *during*.

After the death of John the Baptist, Jesus sought a solitary place to pray. Although delayed by crowds, he made time to draw near to his Father. He often prayed after a long day of ministry. Our brother, the man Jesus, continues to communicate with God after his physical work on earth: "Christ Jesus is the one who died—more than that, who was raised—who is at the right hand of God, who indeed is interceding for us" (Rom. 8:34). His prayers brought renewed focus and energy to his ministry on earth, and his communication with our Father brings the same for winning women today. Jesus prayed *after.*

Jesus told his followers, "The Son can do nothing of his own accord, but only what he sees the Father doing" (John 5:19). Every action, message, and miracle resulted from the direct leading of God. His constant communication fueled his ministry, and Jesus drew from the Father on all occasions. He initiated nothing on his own. If Jesus, the Son of God, saw the all-encompassing need for a committed prayer life, we can settle for no less.

> The value of persistent prayer is not that God will hear us but that we will finally hear him.
>
> Prayer is the greatest of all forces, because it honors God and brings him into active aid.
> —E. M. Bounds

Prayer Commitment

Winning women, the time has come for an ironclad commitment to battle for our families, our communities, and ourselves. Not an "I'll try it." No. Our Father longs for devoted women who will commit to real prayer: "I will pray. I will engage. I will make time. I will intentionally seek God through prayer—every day, always." Can we make this kind of commitment? This may seem daunting because the tomfoolery of the devil suggests we're too busy for committed prayer. Cast out that lie! The enemy leaps for joy when this lie steals from women of God. Communication with God remains one of the best gifts you can give your family, your friends, yourself, and the world.

We will not regret time spent in prayer—we will regret not praying without ceasing.

My Dog Tag
(Fill in Your Name)

"Evening, morning and noon I cry out in distress, and he hears _____'s voice" (Ps. 55:17 NIV).

In the Trenches with Deanna: My marriage was over. After two years of marriage to the cowboy of my dreams, those dreams had morphed into nightmares. We didn't love each other anymore. Indifferent, we didn't like each other. He wasn't the cowboy I married, and I wasn't the bride he took on his honeymoon. I was sick of horses and everything related. Unfortunately, those were his career. By that time, I could no longer remember why I thought cowboys were romantic. Mine just seemed dirty, tired, and broke. Of course, I wasn't a great wife. I worked long hours to avoid going home, spent money on clothes to help my mood, and grumbled constantly about him.

We did nothing to resolve conflict or mend our shredded marriage. We just stayed in a place of awful—roommates who barely tolerated each other. We excelled at causing the other misery. Our marriage was going somewhere fast—divorce court. One day, when we discussed who would keep the dishes, the furniture, and the credit card bills, my heart did an about-face. I had not prayed for this startling change of heart. Selfishly, I just wanted a different, my-way kind of life. Yet, as we sat there dividing our earthly possessions, a voice in my head began screaming, "*Say no to divorce!*"

This voice refused to be quiet or ignored, and it required my cooperation. Years later, I discovered the source of that un-ignorable voice—my mom's prayers. Thankfully, my mother never stopped praying for us (unknown to me at the time). She must have planted herself at God's throne, refusing to move until he invaded her daughter's broken marriage. No other reason exists. I was refusing to make any efforts to save our marriage. I had given up. I saw no other viable solution. Divorce was my only option for escaping the life I hated.

Prayer—and not prayers prayed by me—saved my marriage. God moved mysteriously into our marriage through my mother's prayers. Life came back into a marriage that had died. Troy, my cowboy, and I have been married over twenty years. We are not characters in some fairy tale, but we love each other. We have a dusty, rugged, beautiful, God-filled life. What we now share did not result from our puny efforts—our family is the direct result of faith-filled, *relentless* prayers.

For me, prayerlessness had created a void in my marriage. Prayer draws and pulls in Almighty God, who brings the dead to life and heals the incurable. God did what we could never do in our own power. God's authority, through the power of prayer, overcame our selfish individualism and made us one in our marriage.

Armor of God

(Fill in Your Name)

Sword: "_____, rejoice in hope, be patient in tribulation, and be constant in prayer" (Rom. 12:12).

Shield: "_____, beloved, building [yourself] up in your most holy faith and praying in the Holy Spirit, keep [yourself] in the love of God, waiting for the mercy of our Lord Jesus Christ that leads to eternal life" (Jude 1:20–21).

Shoes: "Make me to know your ways, O Lord; teach _____ your paths" (Ps. 25:4).

The Poverty of Prayerlessness

Without a doubt, those who refuse to pray are impoverished.

Job reveals that the wicked seem to prosper in this world. Full of pride in self and assets, they say to God, "Depart from us! We do not desire the knowledge of your ways," and they add further insult to God by saying, "What is the Almighty, that we should serve him? And what profit do we get if we pray to him?" (Job 21:14–15).

David grew weary of fools, who said there is no God, who do "not call upon the Lord" (Ps. 14:1, 4), who grew so wicked that killing a person was as easy as eating a piece of bread. In a psalm that criticizes the wicked, Asaph calls upon God to pour out his wrath on nations and kingdoms that fail to call upon the Lord (Ps. 79:6–7).

During a sinful time in Israel's history, when they sought a king to rule over them instead of God, the prophet Samuel delivered a warning, a blessing, and a tutorial on prayer. The aged prophet Samuel, endowed with wisdom from above, delivered a persuasive farewell speech to Israel after she had asked for a king (1 Sam. 12:6–25). At God's command, Samuel anointed a king, but Samuel knew Israel would experience the emptiness of turning to a mere man to lead them, when they could have had God as Chief Commander. Within Samuel's speech, the aged prophet also taught about prayer and the true source of completeness.

First, he reminded Israel of God's faithfulness (6–11). Second, he cautioned Israel that both a king and citizens must obey the Lord for peace to reign (12–14). Third, he warned about disobedience—that God's hand would be against them if they disobeyed (15). Next, God demonstrated his power to answer prayer immediately.

Because Israel was wicked in denying God as their king, Samuel told them he would pray for rain on that sunny harvest day, soaking and possibly ruining their entire crop of wheat. After he had prayed, the Lord sent rain and thunder. (Occasional thunderstorms occur during the wheat harvest months of May and June, but they are rare.) The thunderstorm wasn't the miracle, because out-of-season rainstorms can happen. The immediacy of answer to prayer was the miracle, and Israel was convinced that they had heard the voice of God (in the thunder). Through that "power point" lesson, Israel's awe of God and the chosen prophet Samuel increased (16–18).

From the heavens, rain poured upon the hopes of harvest, and thunder rumbled and shook the earth. In Hebrew, the word *thunder* means *voices*.[1] When Scriptures mention thunder, many of them refer to thunder as the voice of God. Israel witnessed

God's immediate response to Samuel's prayer and called upon him to intercede and ask that God spare their lives. They confessed they had added to their other evils by asking for a king.

Samuel didn't let their rejection of him affect his reply, and he spoke comfort, "Do not be afraid" (20), but neither did he slough off their irreverence and sin, "You have committed all this evil, yet do not turn aside from following the Lord, but serve the Lord with all your heart" (20). Then he revealed why God's supremacy is crucial, "And do not turn aside after *empty things that cannot profit or deliver,* for they are empty" (21; emphasis ours).

Empty vanities of the world bring only temporary satisfactions, but sometimes that realization takes many years to reach the heart. Winning women, we hope to hurry that message along to you—that all profit and deliverance are bound up in God's adoption of you as his child, with all the blessings and personal communication through prayer that entails.

Prayer Substitutions

When a woman gets out of sorts, she knows what will bring temporary comfort. She may eat a delectable food or buy a latte. Another might read fiction with a happily-ever-after ending. A stressed mom might fixate on the newest kitchen gadget, with hopes of simplifying her hectic life. Another might turn on the TV every waking hour to fill the emptiness of her home and heart. Others might drink a glass of wine to relax in the evening. Still another might pare down her to-do list, because if the projects are finished, only then could she relax and focus on the important work of prayer.

We say communication with God is important. What does our prayer life say? Richard J. Foster says this about constant prayer: "It is not prayer in addition to our work but prayer simultaneous with work. We precede, enfold, and follow all our work with prayer. Prayer and action become wedded."[2]

Communication with our Father through prayer allows him to become our Potter, the shaper of our souls, adding texture that only his hand can provide. The more we converse with God during the ordinary details of life, and the more his presence becomes real in winning women's lives, the more prayer substitutions will no longer allure us. For he alone perfectly fits the hollow places in our hearts.

In the Trenches with Cathy: I was eager to arrive home, go to a private place, and weep because my heart was about to burst. I had a weight bearing down on my chest like never before. I didn't want my husband in a war zone halfway around the world. His family and I rode from the airport in silence, each member lost in thought. I knew the main prayer lifting from my in-laws' car was safety for their son and my husband of three months. New in our relationships, I can only describe the mood within the car as stoic. I held my tears in check and so did my husband's father, mother, and two sisters.   After the hour ride, my mother-in-law walked me to my parents' door, where I would live until my husband, David, returned from a year in Vietnam. My mother-in-law hugged me and grasped my hand. "I'm sure he will be okay." I knew her words were simply the broken heart of a mother combining her prayers, wishes, and wants into our farewell. Inside, I discovered my parents entertained a couple I'd never met, so I went through courteous introductions while Dad explained where I had been. More people. More polite words. More offers of prayer. More pressure building.

I excused myself and walked to the guest bathroom adjacent to the family room. I slumped to the floor near the tub, rested against it, and wept. Never before had I felt such helplessness. Anguish, dread, and overwhelming sorrow poured out in quiet sobs. Many years later, my sister and I talked about tough times in life, and I named that night as one of mine. "I needed to be by myself and pour out my tears in silence." Meekly she said, "Your tears weren't silent. That wall was thin, and our whole family and the guests heard you crying. We all teared up and you cried a long time. I know our guests felt like they were intruding on private family time and within a few minutes they left."

The night my husband left, I lamented in prayer and tears, but serious prayer remained new to me. As I reflect on that year, I see the upstart of real talks with my Father. The prayer seeds planted between toddler and teen years blossomed. Until the crisis of my husband living in a war zone, praying without ceasing was an unpracticed concept. I prayed for wants occasionally. I said thank you to God sometimes. I prayed for others sporadically.

During those twelve months, the Holy Spirit called me to prayer. The evening news would give alarming casualty updates, and I'd remember, *I haven't prayed for David today*. My husband's faith and prayers prompted more from me, as he wrote in one of his letters: "I'll have a long time to pray for us tonight. That is the only thing I like about walking fireguard, because I have a chance to pray in earnest. I always kneel on the stairs . . . because no one is around to see me." I wanted to match his sincerity, but I wasn't there. Did my prayer life make a total about-face? No. However, that year, God ignited a truth within my heart that he alone sustains through ordinary days or war.

Winning women, we have prayed that God kindle knowledge that he can and will profit your soul and overflow your heart, so you in turn can spill grace upon grace to your family and others. We long for you to turn your back on temporary world fixes. We urge you to pray to the one who knows you and can satisfy every need at exactly the right time. We desire that you carve out a still and quiet time when you rest in prayer and trust that God will bring satisfaction to your soul and fullness to life as he has done for other conquering women throughout the ages.

Combat Mission for This Week
Let prayer be as steady as your heartbeat—
without ceasing.

Historical Field Guide

Two songwriters who lived thousands of years apart wrote about the turmoil of life and that God sustains the weary during such times. A psalmist penned the first hymn, known to us as Psalm 46, and within the verses affirms that "God is our refuge and strength, an ever-present help in trouble," during natural disasters (2–3), political upheaval (4–7), and battle fatigue (8–11). The psalmist plugged in God's own words when he wrote, "Be still, and know that I am God; I will be exalted among the nations, I will be exalted in the earth" (10)—those lyrics, most likely the best known from the psalm.

In the fifteenth century, on November 10, 1483, a baby boy was born to Hans and Margaretha Luder of Eisleben, Germany, and they named him Martin. The man, known as Martin Luther, earned many degrees and would become a known spiritual leader, especially for his Ninety-Five Theses nailed to the door of the Wittenberg church and his later translating and publishing the Bible in the common German language.

In 1529, Luther wrote "A Mighty Fortress Is Our God," often called "The Battle Hymn of the Reformation." During that period of his life, he was translating the Old Testament and in exile because of his Protestant beliefs. His lyrics show he faced real enemies, but he recognized God as his constant and mighty fortress, a place of refuge during danger. The hymn paraphrases Psalm 46, and it became a favorite among Lutherans and Protestants. Oddly enough, even though the hymn was written during some of Luther's fiercest battles with the papacy, the hymn has found a place in *The Catholic Book of Worship*, but not without controversy.

Martin Luther (1483–1546) undoubtedly found great strength in Psalm 46, and he penned his own relevant version to encourage others who would face formidable foes. He particularly focused upon the "Man at our side": "Did we in our own strength confide, our striving would be losing; Were not the right Man on our side, the Man of God's own choosing: Dost ask who that may be? Christ Jesus, it is He."

When we combine the urging of our Father "to be still and know that I am God" with the recognition of the constancy of the "Man at our side," winning women will pray in quietness and confidence, depending upon God's joy and strength to equip us *before* ills arrive.[3]

Combat Prayer

My fickle thoughts often stray from you, Father.

Please, come find me.

I have gone astray like a lost sheep; seek your servant

(Ps. 119:176).

Tactical Training

1. Research the Gospels, and find more of Jesus's prayer times. Were the prayers before, during, or after happenings or events?

2. In Samuel's rebuke of Israel, what was the main evil they committed? (1 Sam. 12). List "unprofitable" things you allow in your life. Why did Israel choose to have a king reign over them? What things reign over or swallow your time and keep you from an audience with the King who can profit your life?

3. Have you ever experienced an immediate answer to prayer as the prophet Samuel did? If so, write a few short sentences about God's quick grace that arrived when you made a request.

4. Do you believe in the power of prayer? Does your prayer life reflect your belief or lack of belief? Identify a specific area of unbelief in your life. Give it to God. He can remove doubts and bolster your faith.

5. On average, how much time do you spend praying daily? Do you spend adequate time in conversation with God? What could you tweak in your schedule, allowing more time for prayer? What will you do today to increase prayer time?

6. Read Psalm 46. The Psalm mentions battle fatigue, natural disasters, and political upheaval. Within it, God says, "Be still, and know that I am God." Do you practice this instruction from God to rest from troubles and busyness and be quiet before him? How do you most often pray: on the run or still in one place?

7. When others grow weak and can't pray, intercessory prayer remains vital. Have you ever experienced a time of prayerlessness because of lack of faith or worry gone wild? How long did it last?

8. Have you ever directly benefitted from the prayers of another? Have you thanked that person for the precious gift of those prayers? If not, send a note thanking him or her and

then spend time thanking God for the person, the prayers, and the answer.

My Diary from the Trenches

Expect your loving Father to call you to stillness in prayer this week. Record your victories.

Chapter Two

Intercession for All People

Abraham

> "And the scripture was fulfilled that says, 'Abraham believed God, and it was credited to him as righteousness,' and he was called God's friend." —James 2:23 NIV

"I'll pray for you," heard often among Christian women, is a promise to step into the gap and pray. When we share about a future event that concerns us, and a friend parts with promises of prayer, we are comforted. How often, outside Christian circles, does someone promise to stand in the gap for you? A job interview, an inevitable move to another state, a first child is due—then several women of God pledge to pray, and immediately you're not alone in carrying your cares to the Lord. Most likely through a lifetime, you will have troops of women who purpose to lift your needs to the Father.

When other women pray for you, they caravan your needs to God. If you immediately think of slow-plodding camels carrying burdens of prayer, please replace it with the image of camels on a zip line. When friends become the go-between to seek God's will for another woman, it's like a conference call to God. Intercessory prayer rings into heaven, and God never puts us on hold. The privilege of intercessory prayer is at least twofold. First, solace arrives for the woman on the receiving end, and second, the go-between woman receives sweet satisfaction to pray for another woman.

"Intercessor" has roots in the Latin word *intercedere*, with *inter* meaning "between" and *cedere* meaning "go."[1] Throughout the Bible, believers pray for the saved and unsaved. When Abraham heard of the coming destruction of nearby city dwellers, he pled for the lives of the righteous. Let's consider his early years, his growth with God, and his journey to passionate prayer.

Abraham's Journey to Belief, Prayer, and Friend of God

God chose Abram (later renamed Abraham), who grew up in an idolatrous home, to establish a chosen people through whom the Messiah would arrive. His father was Terah and he "served other gods" (Josh. 24:2). When God called Abraham to leave his home country and travel to a land of promise, God speaks, blesses, and gives instructions. Abraham believes and God credits to him righteousness. Eventually, Abraham will be called "a friend of God" (James 2:23).

Abraham and God have history and relationship by the time Abraham pleaded for saving the righteous in Sodom and Gomorrah (Gen. 18). Abraham boldly said to God, "Will you sweep away the righteous with the wicked? What if there are fifty righteous within the city?" Abraham continued, "Will you then sweep away the place and not spare it for the fifty righteous who are in it?" (23–24).

God patiently listens and doesn't interrupt Abraham. Talk and listen. Listen and talk. The exchange went both ways as

Abraham lowered the number to forty-five, forty, thirty, twenty, and finally ten. With each lower bid, God verbally agreed to the numbers. As the text later reveals, there were less than ten righteous in the cities. God brought about the destruction he had planned, but he mercifully spared Abraham's family who lived there, provided they fully obeyed God's flight strategy.

When standing in the gap for others, we can follow Abraham's lead whether the need is physical or spiritual: remind God of his faithful character (25), be bold (27), be persistent (27–33), be humble, and acknowledge that God is God (27). Finally, trust that the Lord will cause the right outcome: "And the Lord went his way, when he had finished speaking to Abraham, and Abraham returned to his place" (33).

When we intercede for a woman whose hope has gone limp, who has no more strength to pray, we become one of the links that connects her once more to the reality of faith, hope, and love. "So now faith, hope, and love abide, these three; but the greatest of these is love" (1 Cor. 13:13). Faith, hope, and love always exist in the character of God, but they can seem out of reach and beyond the grasp of those entrenched in war zones. The intercessor links the helpless back to God, affirming her faith, hastening hope, and reminding her of God's love within reach.

Make the habit of intercessory prayer while your family and friends enjoy peacetime. Pray *before*.

> No one is a firmer believer in the power of prayer than the devil; not that he practices it, but he suffers from it. —Guy H. King

> When we pray for others, God listens and blesses them. When you are content, remember someone prayed for you.

In the Trenches with Deanna: My cowboy and I have worked in youth ministry most of our married life, and a few youth burrowed deep into our hearts. God burdened our hearts for these students and created a precious bond. One young man stands out, not for his charming grin or engaging personality, but for the number of prayers spoken for him. Let's just say—trouble had no problem finding Brandon.

He had a fiery temper with an extremely short fuse. He also enjoyed walking as close to the forbidden as possible, and stepping over the line happened far too often. His mom, through a voice choked with tears, regularly asked us to pray for Brandon, and we did. After punching a hole in the wall of his home one evening because of a nasty fight with his dad, Brandon showed up for youth group. His mom had phoned and given me a short version of the explosive altercation. However, when he arrived, there was zero evidence of the hostility. He smiled, charmed, and proceeded as if all was perfect in his world.

Brandon—the charmer full of smiles by day and loads of trouble by night. The situation deteriorated further over time until he could no longer mask the mess inside. He failed the first semester of college, easily done when not attending classes and partying. His parents brought him home and the downward spiral reached alarming speeds.

Already walking close to a steep edge, Brandon went over the cliff when he began doing drugs. His parents kicked him out of the house after every other option was exhausted. He bummed around from one friend's house to another. Brandon wasted a year and a half of his life in the drug world. A local rehab enrolled him, but Brandon never showed for sessions. It was time for something drastic. I got a phone call.

Brandon's mom called and filled me in on a few details and then begged for my prayers. Brandon would leave the state for a special drug rehab program for six months. I called a few girl-friends and asked for a special prayer session for Brandon. With clarity, I recall the four of us on our knees in my living room petitioning God on Brandon's behalf.

"Destroy strongholds!"

"Rescue him!"

"Keep Satan far from him!"

"Guide Brandon's steps and bring him back to you, God."

We made many more petitions that day, and then Brandon was gone and the months passed. We prayed for him regularly, but with no idea how he was doing—and then another phone call. We were invited to a graduation ceremony, and we saw his mom's tears of joy as she watched her son complete the rite of passage that declared him a man, a man of God.

Brandon remained out of state. He wasn't ready for face-to-face encounters with his former companions and temptations. After many years, he returned home and is a man of God—drug-free for over ten years. At this writing, he's scheduled to share his testimony with a youth group.[2]

God, so gracious and good, did far more with those prayers than we could ask or imagine.

The Prayed-Up Life

What would the prayed-up life look like? What will be the focus of your intercessory prayers—*before* prayers— for all people? The New Testament writers urge believers to pray for one another. Paul wrote to the Ephesians, "Praying at all times in the Spirit, with all prayer and supplication. To that end, keep alert with all perseverance, making supplication for all the saints" (6:18).

Jesus said to intercede for your enemies: "I say to you, Love your enemies and pray for those who persecute you" (Matt. 5:44). Paul wrote to the youthful Timothy, "First of all, then, I urge that supplications, prayers, intercessions, and thanksgivings be made for all people" (1 Tim. 2:1). In addition, Jesus taught that we pray God's will be done on earth as it is in heaven. A strong call goes out to believers to intercede for all.

What should we pray? Undoubtedly, we approach God and give thanks for the blessings of family and friends and the ongoing generosity of God, who lavishly sustains and supplies all physical lives. Beyond those, what sort of blessings are we to ask for the population of this earth? God supplies the answer in John 3:16–18, that people come to believe in Jesus, the Son of God.

My Dog Tag

"_____, everyone then who hears these words of mine and does them will be like a wise [woman] who built [her] house on the rock. And the rain fell, and the floods came, and the winds blew and beat on that house, but it did not fall, because it had been founded on the rock" (Matt. 7:24–25).

In the Trenches with Jesus: Before Jesus started his ministry, he prayed and fasted forty days, and before Jesus chose his disciples, he prayed all night. Before the cross, we see him on his face pleading with God. Jesus was a do-ahead person of prayer. Can we be any less?

Even though we don't know his exact communication with God during two of those prayer watches, we can still follow his example and talk to God in *before* prayers. By following Jesus's mode of *before* prayers, we can praise God for the directives he provided and ask for wisdom from above. Every day, and even though we don't know what lies ahead in that day, we can ask for more of the Holy Spirit to affect our hearts and gain glory for God through us. "If you then, who are evil, know how to give good gifts to your children, how much more will the heavenly Father give the Holy Spirit to those who ask him!" (Luke 11:13).

Armor of God

Sword: "Not to _____, O LORD, not to _____, but to your name give glory, for the sake of your steadfast love and your faithfulness!" (Ps. 115:1).

Shield: "Finally, _____, be strong in the Lord and in the strength of his might. Put on the whole armor of God, that you may be able to stand against the schemes of the devil" (Eph. 6:10–11).

Shoes: "The path of the righteous is level; you make level the way of the righteous _____" (Isa. 26:7).

James, the brother of Jesus, said, "If any of you lacks wisdom, let him ask God, who gives generously to all without reproach, and it will be given him" (James 1:5). With stored up wisdom from above and dressed in the armor of God (Eph. 6), our effective *before* prayers help us avoid panicked decisions and wringing of hands. Surely, surprises will come along, but when we are prayed-up, our hearts are prepared for all circumstances. Praying *before* is huge! Jesus showed us how.

In the Trenches with Cathy: On a Tuesday morning, I placed a book about cancer on the front seat of my car, so I would remember to give it to a woman at our congregation on Wednesday, who had been newly diagnosed with breast cancer. Later on Tuesday, I would shop for groceries, so I prayed, "Lord, help me be aware of others. When our paths cross, help me notice if any have needs." It was a simple prayer, not even one I had thought much about before. The plea just sprang forth during those morning prayers.

Later that day, at our local superstore, I put a crossandra plant in my basket that's hearty and has long-lasting orange blossoms. Then I shopped for groceries, and while checking out, I saw a woman exiting the store who also had several crossandra plants in her cart. Immediately, I was on alert, and I asked the Lord in my heart, "Am I supposed to speak to her?" That woman left the store in haste, and she pushed her buggy uphill faster than I can run downhill.

When I couldn't get near enough to speak with her, I consoled myself. "Well, I guess I wasn't supposed to talk to her after all, Lord. Really, I'm not going to chase her down in this heat. She'd think I was crazy anyway." Loading groceries into the back of my SUV, I had barely prayed that consolation prayer, when I heard a female voice behind me say, "I love your hair." I turned around to see a young woman in her mid-thirties and told her, "Thank you."

She reached up and touched the top of the baseball cap that covered her head. "I'm getting my first haircut tomorrow. I've been taking chemo treatments for breast cancer, and my hair has finally grown out enough to need shaping." Within my spirit, I recognized the answer to my earlier prayer. After we chatted back and forth nonsensically about haircuts and hairdressers, I said, "I was supposed to meet you today." She looked puzzled, maybe a bit wary. I asked, "Can you wait a minute? I have a book for you."

After retrieving the book, I handed it to her. "I wrote *Dogwood Winter: Weathering Cancer with Hope* with my late friend, Beverly Grayson, who battled cancer for almost nine years. She was older than you, and the Lord finally took her home, but she poured her faith into these pages, and I know her faith will bless you. This is why she wanted the book published, to encourage people just like you." A pleasant smile wreathed her face as she hugged the book to her chest. "I can't believe this. Thank you." Then she reached out and hugged me.

I returned her hug, saying, "I pray you will be well and that you get a really cute hairstyle!" She walked away with a final thank you, and I finished loading my groceries. Smiling. Smiling. Smiling.

I remain in awe of God and how he answers our *before*, intercessory prayers for others—even strangers.

Combat Mission for This Week

Step into the gap with *before* prayers for another woman, a family, or a country and ask for godly wisdom for them.

———————— Historical Field Guide ————————

Women pray everywhere and at every speed. We pray while driving a car, running after a lost toddler, swimming laps, or collapsing in bed at night. However, when a woman chooses to be still, pray, and know God, she might choose one of the five traditional postures of prayer.

First, in the most practiced prayer posture in the East, people stand with their arms outstretched, palms and eyes open toward heaven. That posture is called *orans* (Latin for praying). In Western cultures, the clergy practices this posture when blessing wine and bread during Eucharist. In synagogues, worshipers stand to pray.

The second posture also finds the petitioner standing, but with eyes closed or averted, with hands clasped at the waist. This was the typical stance of a submissive prisoner. The humble tax collector stood in this posture and "would not even look up to heaven" (Luke 18:10–13 NIV). This posture occurs in many Western churches at the close of corporate worship as the congregation prays.

Third, the kneeling posture was typical when begging a favor from a king or pledging submission or obedience. The eyes could be closed or looking up. This became the traditional posture for reverence, repentance, or requests. In the Latin Rite of Roman Catholicism, it was formerly the custom to kneel on the left knee only, to genuflect, for persons of distinction such as kings, the pope, or bishops. However, worshipers kneeled on the right knee for the Eucharist, when it was enclosed in the tabernacle (a locked box where the bread, the body of Christ, is kept when not in use for communion). Worshipers knelt on both knees when the Eucharist was exposed.[3]

In Jesus's story when a servant begs a master to forgive his debt, the servant kneels (Matt. 18:26). Jesus knelt in the garden as he sought release from his God-assignment (Luke 22:41–44). Some Western churches have kneeling rails to allow worshipers to kneel between the pews. Some have kneelers near the front altar, so congregants can gather to pray or take communion.

Fourth, to pray in a prostrate or prone position, lie on your stomach with eyes averted or closed. This posture became the traditional posture for desperate, repentant, or intercessory prayer. Members of Eastern churches that have plenty of room practice prostrate prayer during services. Also, this posture may happen naturally in private communication with God for urgent pleas, as Jesus did when praying in the garden just hours before his death. "He fell on his face and prayed" (Matt. 26:38–39).

Fifth, the seated prayer posture shows humility; most Western churches sit on a pew with heads bowed and hands folded. Praying while seated became more common with the invention of the church pew. "By the 13th century, backless stone benches began to appear in English churches." Pews became more prominent when the Protestant movement shifted the focus of worship to the sermon, because the sermons tended to be long. Pews became a standard item of church furniture. David sat for prayer as noted in 2 Samuel 7:18.[4]

Whatever posture a winning woman chooses during prayer will most likely depend upon her place of worship, her energy level, and whether her prayers are public or private. The important message in all of this: "Don't Just Stand There. Pray Something."[5]

Combat Prayer
Keep me dedicated to *before* prayers based on your Word.

Oh that my ways may be steadfast in keeping your statutes!
(Ps. 119:5)

Tactical Training

1. Read Genesis 18:16–33. Consider the courtesy and demeanor of God during Abraham's plea. Now read 2 Peter 3:9. What causes God to wait to punish people?

2. Read Esther 4:15–17. Esther asked for an intercessory fast before she went to see the king, but she and her maidens also did the hard work of fasting. Recall her story. Think through her fears. Did she have courage after the fasting and prayer? What was the outcome of their agreed-upon focus?

3. What helps you remember to keep your prayer promises? When you say you will intercede for others, what percentage of those times do you follow through? Try immediately praying aloud or in your spirit instead of simply making a promise that could be forgotten.

4. If your prayer life is minimal, do you ask for prayers from someone who has bold faith and a steady prayer life? What

do you think hinders you from a steady and stronger prayer life? Is it possible to be spiritually lazy and not do the work of prayer?

5. Read Matthew 5:44. Generally, how broad or narrow are your prayers? In the big picture, God's enemies are your enemies. How often do you pray for the world at large to have salvation? When you have prayed for personal enemies, how difficult did you find that? What results did you receive?

6. When women pray for your specific request, do you follow up to let them know results? Do you say thank you? You can be a catalyst to strengthen their prayer lives by giving them a follow-up report.

7. In the NIV translation, read Luke 9:28–32; John 17:1; and 1 Timothy 2:8. What prayer postures are mentioned? What is your most frequent prayer posture? Recall your peace or distress in different postures of prayer. Do you pray more casual or formal prayers? Have urgent needs ever called you to a more humble posture?

8. How important do you think it is to pray for wisdom from above and to ask God for more of his Holy Spirit? What most touched your heart in this chapter about intercessory

prayer? Write the name of one person for whom you can step into the gap and pray in the next seven days.

My Diary from the Trenches

Expect Abba Father to hear and answer your *before* prayers. Record your victories.

Chapter Three

Confession Before Restoration

Nehemiah

> "I acknowledged my sin to you, and I did not cover my iniquity; I said, 'I will confess my transgressions to the LORD,' and you forgave the iniquity of my sin." —Psalm 32:5

"I was wrong." These words might be the hardest words in the English language to say. Yet they are possibly the most needed. Wrongs ignored, hidden, denied, or excused only grow. Unfortunately, ignoring our sins remains the most common response because owning a wrong injures our pride.

Watch a group of girls in a gym full of volleyball players, and the youngest group of girls will squabble over who should have gotten the ball before it hit the ground. No one wants to take responsibility. Finger-pointing and angry words lob and volley on the court. However, a person observing the varsity team sees different attitudes. These girls are more mature and know their sport and responsibilities on the court. When a point is lost, the team hears, "My bad," as the individual accepts and owns her mistake. Her teammates are gracious in forgiveness as pats on the back are generously given. Before teamwork can happen, individuals learn to own up to their mistakes for the good of all.

A woman quenches the Holy Spirit when her sins go unconfessed. This results in an increasing dulling of conscience. When she acknowledges sin, pride takes a blow—humility results. God promises grace to the humble, one of the sweet blessings of confession. When winning women admit a sin, fault, or bad habit to another woman or an accountability group, real transparency occurs and the domino effect happens. Relationships grow. A community results where honesty and openness can thrive. With every confession, we allow God to arm us with the freedom of forgiveness.

In the Trenches with Deanna: "And forgive me of all my sins . . . in Jesus's name. Amen." This was the usual endnote for my bedtime prayers the first half of my life. No specifics mentioned, just a wide brush that swept all my sins away with one stroke. I could then sleep easy, because if I died I'd be with Jesus in a new heavenly home . . . even I couldn't sin in my sleep.

There was no need to list all my failings. God could see all, so he already knew. If I cheated on a test, it wasn't mentioned in my prayers. At that young age, saying "I'm sorry" almost physically hurt. I hated admitting I was wrong. I was far more interested in maintaining my sparkly reputation. Sins were excused or ignored, but oh, I knew they were forgiven, because I always asked for that favor every night before bedtime.

No surprise, none of my sin habits went away. My life stayed its course with a subtle shift away from God. My sins, hidden in the dark places of my heart, could flourish and even invite new sin-friends into the dark party. At twenty-two years old, I found myself mired deep in sin, sin I knew was wrong, but I really didn't care. I no longer attended church, only prayed in extreme emergencies, and continually astounded myself with how far I could sink with no acute feelings of guilt.

As I look back to that time, over twenty years ago, I ask myself, *How did I get there? When did I agree to let my life become that mess?*

I can assure you my life plan did not include this horrid detour into a sin-filled life. I was a good girl until one day I wasn't. I didn't jump off into huge sins first. The decline was slow and steady, and once I felt complacent and comfortable, that attitude hurried my descent downward. I distinctly remember at one especially low place praying to God and asking him to partner with my sin: "Don't let anyone know or let me be caught. Let me continue doing what I'm doing." I wasn't caught; my reputation was still clean to outsiders, but my life was rapidly disintegrating. In that muddy self-made mess, this miserable prodigal daughter eventually looked up.

I didn't want the life my sins had created. So I did all I knew to do. I went back to church, and just like the father in the story of the prodigal son, God was waiting. I didn't walk the aisle and confess my sins to the congregation. I didn't tell a soul other than God for over five years. And that was okay. God heard my cries, my confessions. He took my shame and guilt and brought healing and comfort. Once my sins saw the light of God's love, they no longer held me captive. The chains fell off, and I walked away from the destructive habits I had once embraced. I won't lie. Sin's pleasures put up a valiant fight. The whispered lies continued, offered new fun, and promised to feed my starving ego, but those temptations lost their power because, through *before* confession, I had brought them to the purity and holiness of

God. At the foot of the cross where God keeps all appointments, the Light overcame the shadows and darkness.

I still struggle with sin. I often do what I don't want to do and don't do what I want to do. I can relate to Paul's outburst in Romans 7. I know something now that I didn't know then. Through *before* confession, I can bring those secret sins out of the dark corners of my heart and place them in the healing light of God. God destroys the grip of those sins, and through his grace, I am a forgiven winning woman.

> It is not the criminal things that are hardest to confess, but the ridiculous and the shameful.
> —Jean Jacques Rousseau
>
> Confessed faults are half-mended.
> —Scottish Proverb
>
> The confession of evil works is the first beginning of good works. —Saint Augustine

Light Conquers Darkness

Sin left hidden in the dark grows and collects other sins for company. Darkness, the devil's favored lair, puts women at great risk for defeat. Unfortunately, many sins hide there, unexposed to the curative light of Christ. While sin languishes in that cold dark place, the heart of the sinner grows calloused and then hard.

This proverb proves true throughout the Bible narrative: "Blessed is the one who fears the Lord always, but whoever hardens his heart will fall into calamity" (Prov. 28:14). The Israelites slid into sin by intermarrying with foreign women (God had instructed them against such unions). Soon, these families would worship foreign gods, trusting the man-made images of those gods to save them. In time, they completely turned their hearts away from God. This pattern always led to disastrous consequences. A hardened heart does not realize its jeopardy because God's truth no longer affects or penetrates it.

Paul quotes Israel's prophet Isaiah in the last chapter of Acts. "For this people's heart has grown dull, and with their ears they can barely hear, and their eyes they have closed" (Acts 28:27). At the time, Paul was addressing Jews to whom he was proclaiming the gospel message, but they, because of hardened hearts, could not receive the Good News.

Unconfessed sin weakens and can eventually incapacitate those who were once soldiers of the cross. Satan, cloaked in sin and lies, continually whispers dark messages: *Keep me hidden. Don't tell. No one will ever find out.* Sin will always try to block the path to God, the Way, the Truth, and the Light.

Armor of God

Sword: "Wretched [woman] that I am! Who will deliver _____ from this body of death? Thanks be to God through Jesus Christ our Lord!" (Rom. 7:24–25).

Shield: "But he was pierced for _____'s transgressions, he was crushed for _____'s iniquities; upon him was the chastisement that brought _____ peace, and with his wounds _____ is healed" (Isa. 53:5).

Shoes: "And Jesus spoke to [her], saying, _____, 'I am the light of the world. Whoever follows me will not walk in darkness, but will have the light of life'" (John 8:12).

Nehemiah's Example

Israel, despite repeated warnings, turned away from God. They chose to worship idols and participate in horrendous sin. Prophets sent by God warned the people of their impending doom, but the chosen children of God would not listen, and God meted out his judgment exactly as the prophets had warned. Israel fell into the hands of their enemies. The armies of King Nebuchadnezzar destroyed their cities, took them captive, and leveled the temple of God. Captive, the Israelites dispersed throughout the Babylonian empire. However, after seventy years, just as Jeremiah prophesied, the reigning Persian ruler, King Cyrus, granted some of the Israelites freedom to return to their ancestral home and rebuild.

Almost one hundred years later, Nehemiah was cupbearer to King Artaxerxes, who ruled the Persian Empire. Nehemiah, while employed in Susa, still loved his homeland and worshiped the one true God. When men arrived from Jerusalem, Nehemiah requested a report on the progress of the rebuilding effort. Their response grieved Nehemiah. "The remnant there in the province who had survived the exile is in great trouble and shame. The wall of Jerusalem is broken down, and its gates are destroyed by fire" (Neh. 1:3).

Nehemiah, upon hearing the news, wept and mourned for days. During this time, he prayed and fasted. Recorded in the first chapter of Nehemiah, his petition is that the Lord will hear his prayer. Then he does the unexpected. He confesses the sins of the Israelites as a whole and of his father's house: "We have acted very corruptly against you and have not kept the commandments, the statutes, and the rules that you commanded your servant Moses" (1:8). Nehemiah then continues his prayer, asking God to grant him favor before the king, and God graciously answers yes.

Nehemiah confessed sin before he asked for favor from God or the king. He knew something we need to know—sin creates a breach in our relationship with God. In the areas of our lives where sin resides, God cannot tread because, "Your eyes are too pure to look on evil; you cannot tolerate wrongdoing" (Hab. 1:13 NIV). Sin, ignored and unconfessed, grows and eventually edges God right out of our lives. Nehemiah knew this. His ancestors had allowed this to happen with severe consequences. Nehemiah's *before* prayer of confession bears witness to his wisdom and his understanding of the holiness of God.

Later, after the walls and gates were complete, Ezra read the law publicly to the Israelites. Convicted, they wept over their sins. Nehemiah, convinced of their sincere repentance, declared the day holy to the Lord and instructed the people to stop their mourning and celebrate, reminding them that "the joy of the Lord is your strength" (Neh. 8:10). The need for confession and repentance is absolute, but we can't stay there. Continual guilt and shame accomplish nothing good and are not from the Lord but are weapons of the enemy. After confession, worship and joy result because God graciously forgives, renews, and refreshes. "Come now, let us reason together, says the Lord: though your sins are like scarlet, they shall be as white as snow; though they are red like crimson, they shall become like wool" (Isa. 1:18).

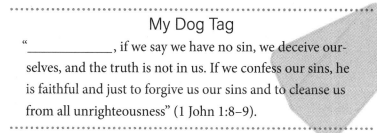

My Dog Tag

"_____, if we say we have no sin, we deceive ourselves, and the truth is not in us. If we confess our sins, he is faithful and just to forgive us our sins and to cleanse us from all unrighteousness" (1 John 1:8–9).

In the Trenches with Cathy: When my family moved to Houston, Texas, and away from rural Arkansas, the grocery store was near enough that my mother would send me to buy a gallon of milk or a loaf of bread. Giving me cash to make the purchase, my parents expected me to go directly to the store and bring the change home. I was eleven, and the oldest child in the family.

Each time I went into the store, I wished to have just five cents to spend on gum or candy because I knew of an only child who got a nickel every day to spend on sugary treats. After months of obediently following my parents' shopping rules, I wondered if my mother would even miss a nickel, and I turned to a life of crime. On several different trips to the store, I spent an extra nickel on gum and stashed the secret supply in my room. Oh boy! This life of criminal activity had sweet rewards. No one seemed any the wiser. Mom didn't even count the returned change. If I gave the coins to Dad, he shoved them in his jeans pocket.

My pleasure was short-lived. I was naïve to think no one would know, not even God. They let my thievery go on one more time just to make sure they were right . . . that I was pilfering from pantry money. When I walked into my home and placed the gallon of milk on the table, mother, busy preparing supper, said, "Give the change to Daddy." My spine prickled . . . a sad tone of voice . . . she kept her back to me . . . what was going on?

I went to the living room, handed the money to Dad, and wished to disappear. Wouldn't this be a swell time for the earth to swallow me whole? Just like that Bible story Mother read to us. Dad held the money in his hand and slowly counted. I prayed for pennies from heaven . . . only five miracle pennies, Lord. I envisioned new striped play clothes with a stenciled number. With a warden's expression, he said, "A nickel is missing. Do you know anything about that, Cathy?"

Somehow, despite my terror at being caught shorthanded, I managed to move my head in a circle that could have meant yes or no, the classic childish maneuver of stalling, deciding if further deception is worth the risk. With no confession coming forth, Dad asked another question.

"Cathy, I'm asking you for the last time. Where is the nickel?"

I was a goner. The end was near. The sky was falling. I'd never date. Never wear lipstick. Never marry. While listening to Daddy, I had memorized the pattern of the tile at my feet. Ashamed, I couldn't look at my hardworking dad, who adored his family and had moved us to Houston, so he could be at home and not work out of town.

I eventually choked out my confession, mainly upset that he'd discovered my ruse. He lectured about deception, how it becomes a lie when a child intentionally misleads a parent. He named my punishment, and then worse than twenty spankings, he told me to go to my room and think about what I'd done. Afterward, I was to go to the kitchen, tell my mother, and say I was sorry.

I have clarity about the moment I walked into the kitchen to confess and apologize to my mother. I can see the chartreuse walls, the darker green tile around the sink and countertop. Mother had on an apron and still had her back to me. She was peeling potatoes at the sink. I stammered, "I'm sorry, and I'll bring home all the change from now on." I added that if I wanted anything extra I'd just ask as Daddy suggested.

That's when she leaned her hip on the counter and turned toward me where I could fully see her. She had tears streaming down her beautiful face, and I knew I had caused them. I felt utter remorse for breaking her heart. Her tears were my undoing. Now, in my later years, I value that as one of our heavenly Father's poignant beginner lessons—sin breaks his heart, too. I didn't at age eleven understand the theology that sin always hurts God first, but I knew an immediate crushing sadness because I had caused my mother sorrow.

Dad was wise to make me go and tell my mother what I had done. I believe the orchestration of confession in the kitchen was God's doing, and the impression helped me prefer right living instead of the misery and the consequences of sin. This *before* confession caused heart growth, necessary before my relationship with Father God could grow.

In the Trenches with Jesus: "If we confess our sins, he is faithful and just to forgive us our sins and to cleanse us from all unrighteousness" (1 John 1:9). When we confess, God forgives. The simple beauty of this grace came at an exuberant cost. We simply allow the Savior to do his work—by exposing our darkness to his redemptive light. We don't have to pay back, work off, or offer a blood sacrifice as wages to cover our sin. In Jesus's *before* prayers, he sought help from his Father to face the dark master of sin and defeat evil, and he did it for us. At the battlefield of the cross, Jesus took on our sins, each and every one of them, and covered them with the blood of his body. Do we realize the price of this indescribable gift and the extravagant privilege our Savior Jesus gave us? Winning women can walk liberated from sin by confessing those sins to our Father who eagerly waits to eradicate them and move them "as far as the east is from the west" (Ps. 103:12).

Confession Before Restoration

Combat Mission for This Week
Ask God to expose any secret sin, confess that sin, and
allow your cleansed heart to accept his forgiveness.

——————————Historical Field Guide——————————

Yom Kippur, also known as the Day of Atonement, is the
holiest day on the Jewish calendar. Only on this day was the
High Priest allowed to enter the Holy of Holies in the temple.
However, since the destruction of the temple in AD 70, this holy
day has changed focus from the temple to the individual. Jews
are by rabbinic tradition called to personal repentance and a
return to God.

On this day, Jews abstain from five forms of pleasure: no
eating or drinking, no washing or bathing, no applying lotions
or perfumes, no wearing of leather shoes, and no marital rela-
tions. The day is spent in prayer with extra services at the synagogue. No physical labor is done on this day. The labor is of a
spiritual nature—in the heart, confessing sins of the year for the
individual.

A special prayer book called *machzor* guides the confession
service at the synagogue. The Jews recite prayers as a congregation. All the people confess both general sins and specific sins
together. According to Jewish law, this is the only day of the year
that sins are forgiven, so it is imperative to confess any possible
sins. The collective prayers conclude with a broad, catchall confession, "Forgive us the breach of positive commands and negative
commands, whether or not they involve an act, whether or not
they are known to us." This is their version of "forgive all my sins."

The concluding service of Yom Kippur, known as Ne'ilah, is one unique to that day. It usually takes about an hour. The ark (a cabinet that contains the scrolls of the Torah) remains open throughout this service, so the assembly must stand in reverence during the prayers. A tone of desperation marks the prayers. The service is often referred to as the closing of the gates, as the "last chance" to get in a good word with God before the holiday ends. The service ends with a very long blast of the shofar (a ram's horn trumpet).[1]

The Jews understand the importance of confessed sin. As we glance back into their history, we can easily understand why. Unconfessed and continual sin resulted in destruction, loss of lives, and exile from their homeland. Unconfessed sin can also cost winning women, destroy relationships, and drive us away from God. But this doesn't have to be our future. Jesus paid for our sins, and confession brings freedom and new life.

My Combat Prayer
Search my heart, God. Expose and remove sin so I can walk in your ways.

Search me, O God, and know my heart! Try me and know my thoughts! And see if there be any grievous way in me, and lead me in the way everlasting! (Ps. 139:23–24)

Tactical Training

1. Are you presently struggling with a specific sin? Read
   Romans 7:21–25. Can you relate to Paul's frustration here?
   Be transparent with God, confess the sin, and ask for his
   grace to overcome it.

2. Read Psalm 51. This is David's cry to the Lord after his sin
   is exposed by Nathan the prophet. Give special attention to
   verses 16 and 17. How do those verses apply to you? Has sin
   ever broken your heart?

3. The first response to sin, as seen in Genesis 3, was to hide
   from God. What causes us to hide? Why does this make
   the situation worse? After God found Adam and Eve, their
   response was to pass blame. Can you relate? Why is it so
   hard to admit our sins?

4. God warns Cain that sin is crouching at his door. He tells
   him, "Its desire is contrary to you, but you must rule over it"
   (Gen. 4:7). What does God want from Cain? How could the
   story have ended differently if Cain had confessed his sin?

5. Read Mark 2:1–12. Why does Jesus forgive the paralytic?
   Which had greater value to the man: healing or forgiveness?
   Why were the scribes offended?

6. Do you have difficulty forgiving others? Is there someone you need to forgive? What keeps you from easily offering forgiveness?

7. Consider James 5:16. Why should we confess sins to one another? What prevents it? Have you ever practiced this and if so how did it turn out?

8. In 1 Corinthians 11:27–30, Paul cautions us to examine ourselves before we participate in the Lord's Supper. What is his warning? Could *before* confessional prayers bring strength to this communion time with the Lord? Write out such a prayer for the next time you meet for communion and place the prayer in your Bible or purse.

My Diary from the Trenches

Expect our Father to call you to confession this week to seek his forgiveness. Record your victories.

Chapter Four

The Gift of Before Signs

Gideon

"And the LORD showed signs and wonders." —Deuteronomy 6:22

Signs—a fundamental part of God's relationship with man through-out time.

He gave Noah a rainbow, Abraham circumcision, Moses miraculous signs, the Egyptians ten plagues. One instruction to Israel, the blood on the doorposts, was a sign for the death angel to pass over that home. The Sabbath was a weekly sign between God and the Jews reminding them of his provision and their trust. Signs continue throughout the pages of the Bible as God used them to confirm messages, show authority, or remind of his goodness.

Signs can be extraordinary or ordinary.

Gideon—Here's Your Sign

Before kings ruled over Israel, God appointed judges for over-throwing enemies and leading his chosen people. Gideon's clan was the "weakest" of his tribe, and he was the "least" in his family according to Gideon in Judges 6. Despite Gideon's perceived shortcomings, a man of God came to Gideon and greeted him. "The LORD is with you, O mighty man of valor" (Judg. 6:12).

The man of God found Gideon hiding from the Midianites in a winepress, beating out his grain. The Midianites had oppressed the Israelites for seven years, stealing their livestock and produce and destroying their land. Gideon had reason to hide, and he didn't look like a candidate for the title "mighty man of valor." He looked like a whipped coward just doing the best he could in an oppressive time. And from the floor of the winepress, which was never intended for separating kernels from chaff, he raised a relevant question. "Please, my lord, if the LORD is with us, why then has all this happened to us? And where are all his wonderful deeds our fathers recounted to us?" (6:13).

Good questions. Why are times so hard? Where are the miracles? Questions we all can relate to and most have asked at one time or another. The man of God didn't defend God or blame the people of Israel. He simply continued by commissioning Gideon, "Go in this might of yours and save Israel from the hand of Midian; do not I send you?" (6:14).

Gideon then listed all the reasons the man should send anyone but him. His balk did not cause God to detour. "But I will be with you" (6:16). A promise and a guarantee. Despite all the excuses Gideon gave to prove he was the wrong man for the job, God's statement trumped all. Who Gideon was did not matter. If God was with him, nothing mattered except for his obedience. And here we hit a snag.

Gideon asked for a sign as proof of who was speaking to him, and then he quickly asked the man to wait while he ran home to get him a gift. The man agreed. Gideon left and returned with a picnic lunch complete with goat-in-a-basket and broth-in-a-pot. The angel of the Lord apparently wasn't hungry, but he didn't let the meal go to waste. He asked Gideon to put the meal on a rock and pour the broth over it. Gideon may have been a little disappointed that his gift sat on the rock, uneaten. But thankfully Gideon simply obeyed and waited. That's when the angel reached out the staff in his hand and fire consumed the meal, and then the angel disappeared.

Gideon in fear and wonder acknowledged, "Alas, O Lord God! For now I have seen the angel of the Lord face to face" (6:22).

The Lord quickly responded to this cry of fear: "Peace be to you. Do not fear; you shall not die" (6:23).

Gideon memorialized the event by building an altar to the Lord there, which he named "The Lord Is Peace" (6:24).

The Lord instructed Gideon to tear down the idols in his town and replace them with an altar for the Lord and offer a sacrifice. Gideon agreed, but because of his fear he obeyed under the cover of darkness. Shortly after this, God set Gideon as leader over Israel's army, and men began to gather to him in preparation for battle. Yet Gideon remained unsure. Despite what he had seen and heard, caution motivated Gideon to ask for a sign from God.

If you will save Israel by my hand, as you have said, behold, I am laying a fleece of wool on the threshing floor. If there is dew on the fleece alone, and it is dry on all the ground, then I shall know that you will save Israel by my hand, as you have said. (Judg. 6:36–37)

"And it was so" (6:38). God did just as Gideon asked and Gideon received his sign. The ground was completely dry, and the fleece was so wet Gideon was able to wring it and fill a bowl with the water. This was not an accident or a freak of nature. This was the sign asked for and a miracle from God.

For whatever reason, Gideon was not completely convinced. So he asked for another sign. "Let not your anger burn against me; let me speak just once more. Please let me test just once more with the fleece. Please let it be dry on the fleece only, and on all the ground let there be dew" (6:39). God gave him that additional sign. Not a "Here's your sign . . . hardheaded or unbeliever," but simply "Here is your sign, I have done as you asked."

From that place of deep trust, Gideon prepared the troops for battle, but God whittled down the army from thirty-two thousand to three hundred. This downsize could have sent Gideon back to his everyday work at the winepress with his grain. However, Gideon now knew, thanks to the signs from God, who was with him. God then gifted Gideon with an unasked-for sign of reassurance. This time, God sent Gideon into the enemy camp to eavesdrop on two soldiers. One soldier told his disturbing dream, and his fellow soldier interpreted the vision sent from God. "This is no other than the sword of Gideon the son of Joash, a man of Israel; God has given into his hand Midian and all the camp" (7:14).

With renewed faith and courage, Gideon returned to his troops with an outrageous battle plan, complete with jars, torches, trumpets, and swords. He split his three hundred men into three groups and spread them out around the Midian campsite. Gideon's attack plan may have seemed ridiculous at first glance, but brilliant in simplicity, it worked. Noise, lights, and an offensive attack, plus the Lord's favor, were more than enough to defeat the army and push them out of Israel.

Later, when Israel asked Gideon to rule over them, Gideon refused. "I will not rule over you, and my son will not rule over you; the LORD will rule over you" (8:23). Gideon, after the many signs and the victory, recognized God's lordship and chose to follow, not lead.

In the Trenches with Jesus: God liberally scattered signs throughout Jesus's time on earth. They began by alerting the wise men of his imminent arrival. They continued at his birth when a host of angels appeared to shepherds in Bethlehem. As Jesus began his ministry, the Spirit of God descended upon him, as God proclaimed, "This is my beloved Son, with whom I am well pleased" (Matt. 3:17). Jesus performed miracle upon miracle during his three-year ministry. All signs, proof of his identity. In John 10, Jesus implored his followers to at least believe the miracles came from God, even if they couldn't believe in him. The purpose of the signs surrounding Jesus was not to create a spectacular show. The signs were there to point the lost, hurting, and needy back to God.

My Dog Tag

"_____, seek first the kingdom of God and his righteousness, and all these things will be added to you" (Matt. 6:33).

Is This the Sign? Go Where?

When instructions come from God, the path may not be bump proof or hazard-free. Just like in Gideon's story, a downsized combat troop or the strategy may seem completely opposite of common sense. Who cuts resources or chooses a fearful leader?

God's ways are not our ways. God does the unexpected, takes the path of *most* resistance, and chooses the least desirable leaders in the eyes of the world. He could be his own "over the top, not what you expect" reality show. Wise winning women will remember this as they seek to follow him.

What is the purpose for God's way? Why travel the long way around? Who chooses the least qualified leader? Really, we must walk the path with potholes? The answers are rooted in who God is: he is love and everything he does comes from that place. While his ways may seem illogical, we can always know the answer is about love—God's indescribable, unexplainable, and inexhaustible love for his creation and his children. God is a personal trainer, and his training develops faith and relationship, both far more valuable than the perceived "easy way."

Winning women hold tight to this truth when the way becomes treacherous: when we seek after God, he uses everything in our lives for our eventual good. If he only called the best among us, where would that leave the rest of us? Throughout Scripture he demonstrates his power working through the average or below average, creating above average results—miraculous results!

If the way seems ridiculous. If you seem underqualified. If it all looks impossible. Then God might be seeking you. Ask for a sign. Ask for open doors, that no one can shut. Ask him to close doors so no one can open (Rev. 3:7). After you ask—watch. Trust God to reveal himself and his will to you. Don't give into the temptation of figuring the path out yourself, and don't brush off your sign as just a random coincidence. Signs come in a variety of ways, and your sign probably won't look like anyone else's. God is infinitely creative, so observe with eyes wide open in expectation for his marvelous revealing into your life and circumstances.

Armor of God

Sword: "_____, commit your way to the LORD; trust in him, and he will act" (Ps. 37:5).

Shield: "_____, I know the plans I have for you, declares the LORD, plans for welfare and not for evil, to give you a future and a hope" (Jer. 29:11).

Shoes: "Make _____ to know your ways, O LORD; teach _____ your paths" (Ps. 25:4).

In the Trenches with Deanna: We needed a new place to do life, a place with room for about twenty horses. The house didn't matter. We could live in a shack. My cowboy had rented stalls from other barn owners for years. The money we paid in stall rental could provide us a place of our own. We prayed. We planned. On paper this worked, if there were no surprises or unconsidered costs. You can see where this is going. Unexpected expenses pop up all the time.

We had said our sign would be if our house sells, then God has a better place for us. Our home was for sale a previous time without any buyers. So this felt like a reasonable sign. My cowboy began conferring with other cowboy friends, looking for wisdom and additional advice. This led to the sale of our home without a realtor. We would keep more of the profit. Surely this was God giving us an okay to move forward.

The work began. We needed property with plenty of space, preferably one with a barn. And the acreage should have a mandatory soil, both sandy topsoil and clay underneath. Yes, the dirt mattered—the house, not so much. So the search began. I could look all day on the web but no matter what I found, it all came down to the dirt. So we would narrow the search by digging small holes as we visited potential ranches with our realtor. The search took some time.

And then we found it. I loved the house, and even better, the dirt was perfect. We wanted more assurance, and the sign we asked for changed. If they accepted our offer, this was the place God had for us. We prayed and waited. The call came. They accepted. No back and forth negotiating needed. Just done. Accepted.

Well, of course we sought one additional sign. Would a lending institution give us a loan for an agricultural exemption property? This proved difficult. By now we were living at my parents' house, over forty-five minutes away and, through God's providence, all our stuff was stored in the house we wanted to buy. It was a tedious wait. Finally, our closing happened, we signed the papers, and the house and the dirt belonged to us.

Now the real work began. We needed a barn, fences, and everything a horse ranch entails. The surprises and unexpected costs reared their ugly heads. We could not afford this. Why had God opened all these doors just to watch us fall flat on our empty pockets? Where had we misheard him? What were we to do now? We had no answers and lots of questions, but my cowboy believed with everything in him, this was where God wanted us. So I hung on to his faith while mine only grew inch by creeping inch.

We have now been on this ranch ten years. God continues to amaze us with his provision. I cannot tell you how many times

I just knew we were going to lose the ranch, our home, only to have money show up from the oddest sources. This journey has been tough—dirt dog tough—but we have also seen numerous signs from God pointing us to him and confirming his leading.

I Need a Sign

Should I marry this man? Do we buy this house? Where should we attend church? Do I take this job? Do we move? Do we stay?

If only we had specific instructions for life, a direct line for instant answers for every decision we need to make, that would make life so much simpler. Right? We would never make the wrong choice. We would always do the right thing. Life would be perfect with no negative consequences for faulty decisions.

As logical as this sounds, it would not make us happy. Having absolute solutions to all of life's struggles seems perfect, but it isn't. We would ultimately fight the tight restraints. God designed us to live in freedom with Christ and have the freedom to choose. He awards us freedom to follow our dreams and passions, those dreams and passions that God plants in our hearts.

Signs have a real place in our walk with God. He uses them to confirm his direction, to point us to him, to move us to a different path, and to show himself faithful. He can direct our steps when we trust him, acknowledge him, and do not try to figure out all the details on our own (Prov. 3:5–6).

However, his leading is not done singularly or primarily through signs—it is done by faith. He often asks us to step out in faith without a clear-cut sign. Many times, he expects us to take a faith-filled plunge into uncharted waters. Our faith pleases God and he rewards it (Heb. 11:6). When we misstep (and we will), we can trust that he can use even our failings for our good (Rom. 8:28).

We do not always need a sign. Maybe we just need a deeper faith and an occasional sign thrown in to encourage us and draw us closer to God and his desire for our lives. When we seek God first, then we can trust him with all details. It is okay to ask for a sign—the heroes of faith throughout Scripture did—but our mission is to walk by faith.

In the Trenches with Cathy: Soon after my son was born, my mommy mind started to think of all the mischief that a growing boy could get into in his toddler years. I thought about the adventures on our farm: fishing at the pond, exploring the two creeks, and avoiding the protective mama cows with new calves. When Russell was about the age of ten, I thought further down the road: driving, dating, graduating, and beyond. These weren't necessarily anxious moments, but I honestly thought I had considered and prayed over most of the challenges a boy might face. Well, I hadn't.

After he turned eleven, and nearing Christmas, his dad casually said one day, "I think I'll buy Russell a hunting rifle this year." Do what? That wasn't in my list of things my son would ever do. My girlie mind had never envisioned him holding a rifle, much less owning one. I could have gone ballistic, but I didn't. I knew this was a rite of passage for plenty of young men. Living in the country brought rifle needs and game hunting privileges.

A year later, when Russell was twelve, he had a bad cold but he asked to go to town with his friend's family. Russell needed rest and I didn't want to expose another family to his germs. (Did you know a sneeze travels at a hundred miles per hour upon exit?) When I said no to Russell, he fumed—the first time I'd seen his anger at that level. He stomped off, and in a few minutes he came back with his hunting rifle and asked if he could go walking on our acreage. Guided by God's wisdom, I knew not to pick a fight with him about the value of staying indoors. I said, "Yes. You can walk around for thirty minutes."

But as soon as he walked noisily out the back door, my mother heart was gripped with fear and the devil tempted me to worry. Here was my twelve-year-old son, angrier than I'd ever seen him, walking out the door with a gun. My stunning fear helps me remember my exact prayer. I stood by our back door and immediately prayed, "Father, Russell is your child. He has your Holy Spirit in him. Please stir your Spirit to remind him of all the lessons he's learned in our home."

The prayer left my lips, and within seconds, the back door flew open, and my now sweet-spirited son stuck his head in the door and said, "Mom, I just wanted to tell you I love you." He left and relief rushed in and praise poured out.

In my dire need, God showed up on the spot and sent a sign of himself and his attention. That immediate answer to prayer caused my trust and faith in God to make one giant leap forward. Whether we receive a sign or not, God works for our good to groom us into the image of Jesus. God's attention and unfailing love goes before us, leads us, and frees us to praise him so that others may see his good works in us and believe in him.

A Sign from God or a Test for God

Every request for a sign does not please God.

During the temptations of Jesus, Satan challenged him, "If you are the Son of God, throw yourself down, for it is written,

'He will command his angels concerning you.'" Jesus warns Satan, "You shall not put the Lord your God to the test" (Matt. 4:6–7).

Later in Jesus's ministry, religious leaders approached him. "And the Pharisees and Sadducees came, and to test him they asked him to show them a sign from heaven" (Matt. 16:1). By this time, Jesus has performed numerous miracles throughout Israel, but the religious skeptics wanted to disprove Jesus as the Son of God. Jesus rebuked them: "An evil and adulterous generation seeks for a sign" (Matt. 16:4).

When is asking for a sign a test and unpleasing to God? Jesus's reply to the religious cynics who questioned him showed that the deciding factor is not the sign requested but the condition of the heart and motives of the person requesting the sign. When unbelief and a hardened heart drive the demand for a sign, then the sign is a test, and an answer should not be expected. However, when women, prompted by faith, humbly seek a sign for God to point the way they should go, this is not a test. God longs to guide women, he longs for them to follow the leading of the Holy Spirit, and he hears and honors requests made from seeking women. "The good person out of the good treasure of his heart produces good, and the evil person out of his evil treasure produces evil, for out of the abundance of the heart his mouth speaks" (Luke 6:45).

As always, it's a heart thing with God.

Combat Mission for This Week
Intentionally watch for signs from God.

————————Historical Field Guide————————

He was born in 1805 just two days before Christmas. His parents, Joseph Sr. and Lucy, would have eleven children, and Joseph Jr. was number five. Joseph Jr. credited his parents with being godly and instilling in him a love and hunger for God. The family often had morning and evening devotions in their home where hymns were sung, prayers were prayed, and Scripture was read. It would seem Joseph Jr. was well-grounded in truth.

At the age of fourteen, Joseph declared he had seen a sign from God, and he shared this message with others. At the age of twenty-five, Joseph Jr. became a leader of his church. Just two years later, he took the title of president of the office of the high priest. He thought of himself as a modern-day Moses, leading God's people. He even penned a book, which he stated was given to him from God and therefore equal, if not superior to, the Bible. This book set up new truths and laws for the church.

Were the signs and dreams Joseph Smith based his life and his church upon real and were they from God? Was it all a hoax? Truth or lies? When speaking of signs, it is imperative to consider if the message is from God. How do we know? If the person seems like a godly person, shouldn't his or her message be godly? Not always. Discernment, given by the Holy Spirit, should always be called upon. God will *never* direct us to do something contrary to his Word or character. He remains the same yesterday, today, and forever (Heb. 13:8).

Joseph Smith Jr. began the Church of Jesus Christ of Latter-day Saints. That group now claims 15,634,199 members with 30,016 congregations around the world. However, with just a quick look into the Book of Mormon, the reader quickly finds things that are in opposition to the Bible and the character of God.

Alert women seek to follow God and to be aware of wolves in sheep's clothes and messengers of Satan dressed as angels of light. The only way to distinguish lies or truth is to know Jesus, "full of grace and truth" (John 1:14), and then the counterfeit becomes increasingly clear. As we study Scripture, the truth of God's character becomes more obvious. As our relationship with Jesus grows, so does our ability to follow his leading—through his Word, his signs, and the Holy Spirit who resides in us.[1]

Combat Prayer

Lord, open and close doors in my life, so I follow only you.

What he opens no one can shut, and
what he shuts no one can open (Rev. 3:7 NIV).

Tactical Training

1. Do you have your own "in the trenches" story, a time where God opened a door and you entered? Was the way hard? Did you doubt your choice? What was the outcome? Are you still waiting?

2. Think about the heroes of faith. Can you remember signs they may have asked for or received? What was the purpose of the sign? How do these forerunners in the faith encourage you in your walk?

3. Romans 8:14 says the children of God are led by the Spirit. What does this look like? Consider Galatians 5:22–26. Does this passage shed light on what a Spirit-led life looks like?

4. Consider the "I am" statements of Jesus in John 6:35, 8:12, 10:9, 10:11, 11:25, 14:6, and 15:1. Can you relate to any of these? Which one meets you right where you are? Which one do you struggle with? What can you do to embrace these statements from Christ?

5. Read 2 Corinthians 11:3. As we follow the Shepherd, what possible deceptions interrupt our walk with God? How do we avoid or defeat those snares?

6. John 10:27 tells us the sheep that belong to Jesus hear his voice and know him. What does his voice sound like? What doesn't it sound like? How do we grow to hear his voice over the chatter of the world?

7. Have you ever really needed a sign from God? Did you get one? If yes, how did it help you? If no, what did you do? Would you be willing to ask God for a sign in the future? What would be the value and purpose for asking?

8. Read Exodus 17:1–8 and Matthew 16:1–4. What would "testing the Lord" look like in today's world? What could it look like in your life? Pray for God to help you recognize if you ever come close to testing the Lord. Ask for wisdom to overcome this trap.

My Diary from the Trenches

Expect God's guidance this week. Be alert to his leading. Record your victories.

Chapter Five

Valid and Heartfelt Before Requests

Zechariah and Elizabeth

> "When you pray, go into your room and shut the door and pray to your Father who is in secret. And your Father who sees in secret will reward you." —Matthew 6:6

Women pray many *before* prayers for necessities and abundance, continually asking God for kindnesses—both tangible and spiritual. We pray for a mate or ask if singleness be our path. We pray before weddings, bearing children, and rearing children, and then we ask for spiritual growth in our families. If single, we pray that our lives honor God, that he keep us upstanding and moral in a wayward world. We pray before elections. We pray before the start of a new job, a trip, or a school year. We pray when special tasks lay ahead such as budgeting, relocating, or caregiving for parents. We pray valid, heartfelt prayers for the good blessings of life.

We ask because we believe and trust Jesus—that those who ask in faith receive. "Therefore I tell you, whatever you ask in prayer, believe that you have received it, and it will be yours" (Mark

11:24). We women aren't that different from Eve, Hannah, Huldah, Elizabeth, or Lydia, Bible heroines who lived centuries before us.

The Heartfelt Prayers of Elizabeth and Zechariah

Elizabeth's and Zechariah's *before* prayers help us understand the beauty of the righteous desires of the heart (we assume Elizabeth joined her husband in praying for a child). Even though this was the desire of their hearts, both of these descendants of Aaron of the tribe of Levi remained childless into their senior years. Zechariah's name meant, "YAHWEH remembers," while Elizabeth's meant "the oath of God." Soon after their marriage, their community realized Elizabeth was not conceiving. The Jewish people had adopted the notion that a barren woman had sinned grievously against God, and her plight of no children was punishment from God. Perhaps the disdain came about because the Old Law clearly stated that when Israel obeyed God, none of their men, women, or cattle would be barren or miscarry: "You shall be blessed above all peoples. There shall not be male or female barren among you or among your livestock" (Deut. 7:14).

Luke, guided by the Spirit of God, records the truth about Elizabeth and Zechariah. "Both of them were righteous in the sight of God, observing all the Lord's commands and decrees blamelessly" (1:6 NIV). Doctor Luke stated simply that Elizabeth was unable to conceive, and they were both very old (1:7). Unknown to them, their infertility was temporary. They remained childless until the appointed time for the forerunner of Christ to arrive, until God's divine purpose and plan enmeshed their lives with the greatest story of all.

We only know of their prayers through the angel Gabriel's message as the elderly Zechariah stood to the right side of the altar of incense and prayed the usual prayers for Israel. Gabriel said, "Do not be afraid, Zechariah, for your prayer has been heard, and your wife Elizabeth will bear you a son, and you shall call his name John" (Luke 1:13).

We have no way of knowing if God stored Zechariah's prayers for an heir or if he prayed continually into his old age for a child. We wonder if Zechariah quit praying for a child when the wrinkles in his brow increased. Did he stop his prayers for an heir when the couple's physical passions paled and Elizabeth's hair had grayed? If they had stopped praying, God had stored his and her earlier prayers for a baby. They had prayed valid, heartfelt prayers that fit God's will for married couples. When we lay our requests before God, if he answered all of our prayers immediately or within our preferred timing, he would perform his mighty deeds in the framework of our wisdom and whims. Now that's frightening!

As Zechariah stood at the altar of prayer in the temple, did he pray anew, remembering Abraham and Sarah, Isaac and Rebecca, Jacob and Rachel, and Elkanah and Hannah? The Lord God had granted these couples' requests for a child, but always on his ordained clock.

Matthew Henry says in commentary, "Prayers of faith are filed in heaven and not forgotten." And he adds to that, "Prayers made when we were young and entering into the world, may be answered when we are old and going out of the world."[2]

The tick tock of heaven doesn't always sync with the clocks of earth. At heaven's appointed time, God answered this couple and their prayers with a resounding yes. Imagine aged Elizabeth's joy as she awaits the birth of her firstborn in her declining years. Luke recorded an almost audible sigh in Elizabeth's sweet relief.

"Thus the Lord has done for me in the days when he looked on me, to take away my reproach among people" (Luke 1:25). Oh, the joy that leaps into our souls when the Lord turns his face toward us. An indescribable peace descends when, without a doubt, we know his favor rests upon us because he granted a valid, heartfelt request.

Armor of God

Sword: "Yet the LORD longs to be gracious to you; therefore he will rise up to show _____ compassion. For the LORD is a God of justice. Blessed are all who wait for him!" (Isa. 30:18 NIV).

Shield: "Let the words of _____'s mouth and the meditation of _____'s heart be acceptable in your sight, O LORD, my rock and my redeemer (Ps. 19:14).

Shoes: "Who is wise? Let them realize these things. Who is discerning? Let _____ understand. The ways of the Lord are right; the righteous walk in them" (Hos. 14:9 NIV).

In the Trenches with Deanna: The honeymoon seemed like a great time and place to get pregnant. I wanted a baby. All of my childhood dreams included me in the role of mommy. However, my cowboy had very strong opposing opinions. So I began to pray. I wanted a baby at just the right time, when my cowboy and I were both ready—according to God, not according to me. Of course, for some unknown reason I was confident God saw things my way and would change the stubborn cowboy's mind. To my bewildered shock, it didn't work out that way at all. The complete opposite happened. My desire to have a baby simply moved to the back of my mind.

Several years later, my cowboy was ready, but I was not. At my job I was on a fast track to the top and I had no desire to exit the train. Again I prayed for God's perfect timing and this time my cowboy's desire dimmed. After about five and a half years of marriage, we both wanted a baby. God's timing had arrived! Now I simply had to wait for the baby and all the fun baby things. I couldn't wait. The word "excited" was inadequate to describe my emotions. I stocked up on pregnancy tests and bought the required book, *What to Expect When You're Expecting.*

I counted days and took my first test days early. I watched that stick—willing the two lines to appear. And they did! It was faint, but they were there. I was pregnant! And since no part of me is shy, I told everyone I knew plus people I didn't know. I even bought a red bow for her hair (I was confident this baby was a girl). This was the baby I prayed for all those years ago. Or at least that is what I believed.

When I started spotting and cramping, I was so confused and felt sure this was normal. I was only a few weeks along; my body was simply adjusting. But that lie did not last long. When the cramps intensified, the doctor sorrowfully explained what was happening.

I spent the entire day locked in my room—alone. Nothing and no one could comfort me. I was losing my baby, the baby I had prayed for and the baby I thought God had gifted to me. All my *before* prayers seemed wasted and ignored. I could not imagine enduring this emotional pain again. I determined, with a broken heart, that babies just weren't in our future. I mourned my loss and my bleak future for months. My cowboy wanted to try again but I was resolute. *No!* The pain was still too fresh and too consuming.

But again God intervened—this time as the result of my cowboy's current prayers and all those *before* prayers from years ago. As my friends began to get pregnant, the desire for a child stirred in me again. I was frightened, but I was willing to trust God and try again. While I may never understand the "why" of that miscarriage, I do know God heard my *before* prayers, and he answered them. I have two beautiful children who both showed up in our lives at perfect times.

> In repentance and rest is your salvation, in quietness and trust is your strength. —Isaiah 30:15 NIV
>
> Men plan and God laughs. —Yiddish Proverb

In the Trenches with Jesus: Within the Lord's Prayer, Jesus teaches basic and simple communion with God for valid and heartfelt needs. But the simple phrases often carry weighty significance. "Give us this day our daily bread" calls us to deep reliance on our hallowed Father in heaven.

First, Jesus's request for daily bread models basic reliance on God for nourishment of the body. Second, we acknowledge that all grain sprouts at his command and makes its way to our bakeries and pantries because of his generosity alone. Third, we learn to ask for enough, not more or less, toning our desires to daily needs similar to the manna time clock of the desert when they had enough for one day and trusted God for their next meal. Fourth, we acknowledge God's numbering of our days, that he alone knows whether we will even need bread tomorrow.

Finally, by asking God to supply the bread, we acknowledge that we will work honestly to gain bread, never by deceit.

"Give us this day our daily bread"—compelling, bowing-the-knee words that place God at the helm of every breath and every morsel.

When did the phrase "if the Lord wills" disappear from our conversations and prayers, when it was a vibrant fiber of Jesus's being and a verbal part of his prayer in Gethsemane? Maybe it's not left your vocabulary, but we are not hearing it as much. When a family would talk of an upcoming vacation, they shared the itinerary, and then the dad would say, "If the Lord wills." By saying that, he affirmed that if their plans matched God's, then the intended trip would happen. This is a *before* prayer phrase. When a member of a congregation became ill, a petitioner in corporate worship would pray for healing and submit to God's sovereign will by saying, "Your will be done."

Jesus's brother James wrote, "Come now, you who say, 'Today or tomorrow we will go into such and such a town and spend a year there and trade and make a profit'—yet you do not know what tomorrow will bring." He further said, "What is your life? For you are a mist that appears for a little time and then vanishes. Instead you ought to say, 'If the Lord wills, we will live and do this or that'" (James 4:13–15). Why is it important to keep the essence of that phrase in our hearts, conversations, and prayers? Because when we continue, audibly or in our hearts, to acknowledge a truth, that truth becomes part of our being.

James also wrote about wrong motives in our prayers. "You ask and do not receive, because you ask wrongly, to spend it on your passions" (4:3). In some areas, we know the will of God—he has ordained that the seasons remain until the end of time.

We know his will that all must come to him through Jesus. We expect and know that death comes to all men. We know certain unchanging truths. However, when we start thinking we can predict God's will and make absolute plans and they will happen, that's when we live lives of assumptions.

We cannot predict the future. The what, when, where, and how of our lives always rest in tomorrow, in God's vault of sunrises, not ours. Everything depends upon his supply of food, clothing, and drink (Matt. 6:30–33). Jesus came before all things and holds them together (Col. 1:17). God arranges the futures of countries and continents (Ezek. 14:12–14). Doppler radars and meteorologists are only predictors, not God (Job 38:22–24). Dire or robust, economic futures abide in God's domain, such as when he changed Samaria's poor economy for better overnight (2 Kings 6:24–33). When and how each of us will pass from this earth into the hands of God remains in his knowledge, not ours (Dan. 3). Abraham Lincoln said of the future: "The best thing about it, it comes one day at a time."

God alone holds the future in his hand, and we're happy he does, for we dare not trust ours to anyone else. Check your heart motives before you pray. Are you truly satisfied for God to take the lead and his will be done in your life? For better heart habits, instead of saying "Amen" at the end of your prayers, try repeating Jesus Christ's closing words to the Father: "Not my will, but yours, be done" (Luke 22:42).

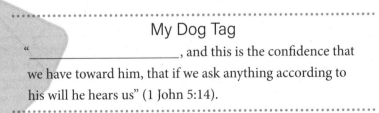

My Dog Tag

"_____, and this is the confidence that we have toward him, that if we ask anything according to his will he hears us" (1 John 5:14).

In the Trenches with Cathy: A man had proposed to me . . . well, he hadn't actually asked yet, but he had suggested marriage when he was a bit angry with me. Not really an argument but more of a disgruntlement had occurred between us, and he said, "Don't you know that I want to marry you someday?" Yes. I had suspected. I had entertained thoughts of marriage. Okay. I had planned the bungalow and the white picket fence—even planted morning glories on a trellis. A girl's imagination will do things like that.

While a preteen, I had only fantasized about marriage, but not the particular man who would put his feet under my breakfast table. Until this man mentioned the big "M" word, my thoughts had remained in fantasyland with a house, children, a cat, a goldfish, and happily-ever-after, but the groom was missing.

About to enter my twenties, the wispy dreams of a young girl had vanished quickly, and the reality of making a good choice for a lifetime-husband descended in a hurry. For days, I thought of the future with this particular man. He was a Christian, a faithful employee, studious in college, obedient to his parents, smart, talented, loyal, and devoted to me. He had the best sense of humor of anyone I'd met, and it was what had first attracted me to him. We had fun when we were together. I could imagine a future life filled with laughter and the joy of the Lord with this man.

As my youthful constructed fairy tales slowly dissipated, a real question surfaced. *Is he the one?* For days, I imagined various scenarios of real marriage to him—our extended families, his chosen occupation, where we would live, his character, his moral choices—but I was hosting a wrestling match between facts and hadn't included holy God in the matchmaking. My spirit was in true turmoil, and I wanted divine help for the answer I would give this man because I sensed a real proposal was near.

One evening, the weight of not having an answer pressed deeply on my heart. I ran water for a bath, and I remember that tears started to fall because of the weighty question "Is he the one, Lord?" The bathroom became my closet, and God saw into that secret place and my confusion. I continued to weep and ask for guidance. At some point in that *before* prayer, my spirit settled. A peace entered my heart. The doubts fled. I knew. I could say yes when he formally asked me to marry him.

During that prayer, God's comforting presence assured me. I have not forgotten that sweet time with my Father and seeking his wise counsel. And God was right. When David Messecar eventually proposed, I said yes with full assurance that our marriage had approval long before we would sign the marriage license. I knew God had heard my *before* prayer and given me an answer, and that pivotal moment of prayer remains a strong memory.

Did we have further disgruntlements? Yep—there have been a few. Bliss every day, are you kidding? We live in the real world the same as other married couples. I love him dearly and have a loyal champion, who regularly tells me he adores me. He refers to me as his bride in public, and he loves me as Jesus loves his bride, the church. If danger were to come my way, I have no doubt that he would lay down his life for me. We have almost fifty years of sliding our feet under the same breakfast table, and there's no one else I'd rather eat jam with or be with in a jam.

Combat Mission for This Week
Request God's grace to accept his purpose,
plan, and timing for your life.

Historical Field Guide

Early Christian art decorates catacombs located on the old road *Via Salaria* in Rome, Italy. The portrayals include the Madonna and Child, Daniel in the Lion's Den, Jesus at the Last Supper, and Jesus the Good Shepherd feeding his sheep. Many other paintings represent heroes and divine intervention. A repeated scene in the funeral art, frescoes, and religious icons depicts an Eastern woman standing with her arms lifted and her palms turned toward the heavens, called *orant* (from Latin for prayer).

One of the more famous artworks of a woman praying in the orant posture is in the Catacomb of Pricilla, in what used to be a stone quarry in antiquity. The walls, ceilings, and tombs display art that families chose to memorialize their beloved. One work shows a woman draped in a deep burgundy robe, arms outstretched to the side, palms up, and her eyes open praying to her heavenly Father. Another family chose to remember a prayerful Egyptian woman on her funeral stele, a monument usually taller than it is wide. A carving shows her standing in the orant posture, arms outstretched in prayer.

While the artwork fascinates us, the most moving thing is that the art represents real women who lived and poured their hearts out to a loving Father who heard their ancient prayers. Perhaps they even prayed for future generations of believers as their Lord Jesus did. Maybe you were on the minds of these ancient sisters in Christ. Will you pray for future generations? Will your family remember you as a woman of prayer?[3]

My Combat Prayer

Lord Jesus, match all my valid requests to your perfect will.

Do not be conformed to this world, but be transformed by the renewal of your mind, that by testing you may discern what is the will of God, what is good and acceptable and perfect. (Rom. 12:2).

Tactical Training

1. List some of the valid, heartfelt requests that women might pray in a lifetime. Have you prayed a pivotal prayer and received an answer that changed or set the course of your life?

2. Read Exodus 23:25–26 and Psalm 107:38. These verses depict God's blessings of fertility for his people, their herds, and their land. Were those general statements or absolute statements?

3. When you prayed and didn't get an outcome you had requested, how difficult was it to accept God's will? Have you ever found out that God's foreknowledge and will was

the best outcome? Have you ever thanked God for saying no to a request?

4. Sovereign God's plan and purpose were not public reproach for Elizabeth. Her censure came from those who dared pass wrong judgments. How can we better embrace the truth of "if the Lord wills"? Could that embedded truth keep us from judging the outcome of others' lives?

5. Read Romans 15:31–32 and Acts 18:21. How did Paul express his plans? Did he give a qualification or condition? How often do you hear the phrase "if the Lord wills" from younger women or senior women? How likely are you to incorporate that language into your conversations and prayers?

6. The following Scriptures shed light on death and God's will about illness and death, the way he recues us from this earth. Read Exodus 21:12–13 (accidents); Isaiah 57:1–2 ("devout people taken away"); Philippians 2:25–27 (Epaphroditus's severe illness and healing); 1 Kings 14:1–13 (King Jeroboam's son died, the only good person in king's family). List your thoughts about God's control of our destinies.

7. Heartfelt and valid prayers will receive a variety of answers. In 1 Thessalonians 5:18, what does Paul encourage us to do, no matter the outcome?

8. While forming better habits of *before* prayer, have you practiced being still, trusting God's will, and praying throughout your day or night? What has surprised you about prayer lately?

My Diary from the Trenches

Expect God to hear your valid, heartfelt prayers that include "not my will, but yours, Lord."

Record your victories.

Chapter Six

Intercession for God's People During Crises

Moses

> "So Moses returned to the LORD and said, 'Alas, this people has sinned a great sin. They have made for themselves gods of gold. But now, if you will forgive their sin—but if not, please blot me out of your book that you have written.'" —Exodus 32:31–32

Has another woman ever asked you to pray for her when her life was ripping apart at the seams? Most of us have had requests from our companions when they are in need of starch and alterations. When physical or spiritual emergencies arrive, winning women of God call upon each other to intercede. Our love for each other runs deep, similar to our brother Moses's, who grew to love God's people so deeply that their suffering and failures pierced his very soul.

Moses's Prayer Struggle and Growth

With God's help, Moses eventually became Israel's most noted leader, and despite his reluctance when first called by Yahweh, he grew to love God with all his heart, mind, and strength, and he selflessly loved his fellow Israelites. Moses learned to promote others above himself. That mark of holiness and humility became Moses's crowning characteristic, revealed in his prayer conversations with God (at least fifteen were recorded in Genesis through Deuteronomy).

When we step into Moses's nomadic life at the ripe age of eighty, we find a settled man. He has run the gamut of life, from a dream palace to his current tent dwelling where he lives a static existence. Let's consider the contrast of his first meeting with God and his later walk with God.

While minding his own sheep, Moses spied an unusual sight: a small bush was on fire and yet the leaves didn't curl or turn to ash. Curious, he moved closer, and that's when he heard a voice, "Moses, Moses"—a personal invitation—but to what? God told Moses to take off his sandals for he was standing on holy ground. During this initial conversation, Moses hid his face, afraid to look at God. Much later, after witnessing God's miraculous care for himself and the Hebrew people, Moses became comfortable with God. That's when the landscape of his prayers changed. From a trembling, face-hiding man, Moses evolved into a man with whom God spoke as a friend, face-to-face (Exod. 33:11). In further meetings with God, Moses's face even reflected God's radiance: "Moses did not know that the skin of his face shone because he had been talking with God" (Exod. 34:29). Moses's conversations with God transformed from hiding his face to being fully present with God, absorbing God's love for people and his radiance. Within that time frame of the burning bush and delivering the chosen people to the borders of Canaan, Moses prayed intercessory prayers. Interceding for others changes us as we experience God's presence and partnering with the desires of his heart.

Most believers struggle to gain understanding about God, to deepen their relationships with God, and to pray within God's will. Women struggle to know what to pray, how to pray, and even when to pray. However, when we persist in seeking the face of God, we sequentially become acquainted with God's purity, holy nature, and desires for all mankind to be saved. As our faith, trust, and knowledge increase, we more fully recognize God as Redeemer, and he places in our hearts a longing for others to know him.

During the long ordeal of the release of Israel from Egyptian bondage, Moses worked in tandem with God. God was chief commander of the exit, and he orchestrated the departure to relieve the oppression and also to gain glory for himself. Moses witnessed God's work, trusted God's promises, and followed God's lead. After the Exodus, we see Moses lie prostrate before God for forty days and nights, and even offer his own soul if God would spare wayward Israel. His intercessory prayers during the crises of their rebellions swayed God, and the intended destruction of Israel didn't occur. Moses's believing, *during* intercessory prayers moved the Creator to repeatedly give a stiff-necked and stiff-hearted people further opportunities to repent and obey.

Like Moses's fixed life in the desert, our prayers can get into a rut. We can drift into praying for physical comforts or dismissal of problems almost to the exclusion of praying for the welfare of souls. In Moses's latter years, he modeled walking gently with God, learning the heart of God, and praying for people's deepest needs.

God Bless Us, Every One

Winning women, Moses's story that changed even at the age of eighty assures us that God will always give us enough time and stamina to complete his missions and purposes for us (Deut. 34:7). As we discovered in Chapter One, we have a mission to pray intercessory prayers for God's people and our enemies and to pray that all the population of earth have opportunity and time to know God. And we pause here to ask ourselves and you a poignant question: If your prayers were divided by percentages, how much time do you pray for your family, friends, enemies, or the lost? After our truthful examination, we saw a lopsided percentage of time spent praying for those we love most dearly. And yet, God sent his son because "God so loved the world. . . ."

As Jacob wrestled with an angel all night to receive blessings, conquering women will wrestle in prayer for another's struggle with sin, an illness, poor finances, bad decisions, marital problems, or prodigal children. Crises crisscross this world every day, and when we hear of them, we are prompted to intercede for people in specific locales because of evil leaders, moral declines, famines, health pandemics, weather crises, and terrorist attacks. Our hearts, after God's own heart, will cause us to pray for the oppressed.

To better plead for others, recall the darker times in your life and be alert to others experiencing the same ailments or sins. You will have keen insight as to what to pray for those who stumble down a path you formerly walked. A recovering drug addict understands the constant fight to not give in to satisfy chemical cravings. A former chemo patient better knows how and what to pray for cancer patients. A porn addict recognizes the fight to keep her mind pure. The woman who struggles with controlling her anger realizes the damage a tirade can trigger. Those who have experienced apathetic faith can pray for women who are adrift in a sea of don't-care and giving-up.

Andrew Murray said, "Each time, before you intercede, be quiet first, and worship God in His glory. Think of what He can do, and how He delights to hear the prayers of His redeemed people. Think of your place and privilege in Christ, and expect great things!"[1] Think of what Christ has done and what he can do, and then examine to see if you have trust issues with God. Our ancient sisters, who moved from slavery to freedom, experienced unparalleled trust training in the desert. For several million people, he provided bread and water and clothing and sandals for forty years until he brought them into a land that could sustain them. In the desert, the homemaker, the cook, the pregnant woman, the preteen, the teenager, and the granny bedded down each night with nothing visible to sustain them. They kissed toddlers good night, knowing they had nothing to feed them in the morn. Wives made love to their able-bodied men in the evenings and totally trusted that God would provide food for their male protectors when the sun arose.

Armor of God

Sword: "_____, may the Lord direct your heart to the love of God and to the steadfastness of Christ" (2 Thess. 3:5)

Shield: "For I, the LORD your God, hold your right hand; it is I who say to _____, 'Fear not, I am the one who helps you'" (Isa. 41:13).

Shoes: "_____ will run in the way of your commandments when you enlarge my heart!" (Ps. 119:32).

Could we pass that test of trust? Could we for forty years go to bed with totally empty pantries and bank accounts and fully believe that the morning dew would bring manna straight from the hand of God? Assess your trust. Do you have an empty pantry, forty-year trust?

In the Trenches with Deanna: We needed a miracle. My mom called way too early one morning, in tears and frantic. There had been an accident. *My cousin. Chris. Shot. Not sure if he would make it. Come now.* All these words swirled around in my head, each fighting for my attention. I cried. I ranted. I begged God. We needed a miracle.

Chris was larger than life, nineteen years old, only nine months younger than me. We were babies. Each just starting our lives. He was home for the summer from college, where he had a full ride scholarship playing baseball. I spent many summer evenings sitting on hot bleachers watching him play his favorite sport. It is what we did—summers with the cousins. I dated his friends and he flirted with mine. It was a sweet arrangement. Cousins are awesome that way.

And now he was fighting for his very life. The details were hazy, but one fact was see-through clear. God had to do something. When I walked in his hospital room and saw all the machines, tubes, and wires, my heart shattered. I was not ready to tell my friend, my cousin good-bye. The prayers flowed. I begged. I made deals. I explained to God why he must do this. I reminded God of his many healings throughout the New Testament. I knew God *could* do this, but I wasn't convinced he *would*—that small variation of just one letter was my undoing.

You see, I knew all about God. I was raised on a pew. I knew my Bible and knew what God could do. However, at this young age, I had not seen much personally. I had prayed for both of my grandparents during their fights with cancer and they both died. All I could think was surely God would say yes this time. Chris was so young and so many people were praying. And so many people who loved him would be crushed by his death.

Despite all my logical reasons for God to say yes to my prayer, he said no. Chris died and a part of my faith died with him. I was so angry and so hurt. I judged God's actions and found him guilty. I was not just hurt. I was offended with God. This loss of faith sent me reeling; the result of that spiraling mess was a life void of prayer. I shut down all communication with God. From my perspective, prayer didn't work. Pray just got your hopes up and then when nothing happened, you had that much farther to fall. After Chris's death, when people asked me to pray for them, I laughed and said, "My track record's awful . . . you don't want my prayers."

Thankfully, God did not let me rot in this pit of prayer-lessness too long. At just the right time, he brought a spiritual mother into my life—Rose. She was (and still is) an incredible woman of prayer. She helped me overcome my fear of prayer and helped me realize a very important truth: prayer matters because the one praying goes into the presence of God, always the perfect place. She also taught me the importance of trusting God even when I did not get my way.

As I began to intercede for others again, I still got plenty of nos, but I also became more aware of the yeses. My faith no longer rested in getting my way because it took root in the Way, the Truth, and the Life! Our responsibility as winning women is prayer—we leave the answers to God, trusting his goodness above all else.

Trust and Pray with Your Eyes on God

Moses's actions and prayers proved his trust in God to direct the path of Israel. Exodus 17:1–7 shows Israel arriving at Rephidim, a waterless place. There, God tested Israel's faith in his provisions, and the Israelites grumbled to Moses, saying he had brought them out into a desert for animals and people alike to die of thirst. Moses called out to God that the people were "ready to stone me." God's convicting answer to Moses: "Walk on ahead of the people." Turn your back on millions of grumbling, thirsty, and even bloodthirsty people. You, Moses, turn to me.

The same principle is true for us when we intercede for bitter and warring people. When we mediate for the desperate and disillusioned, our trust belongs in God, not on personal harm or problematic crowds. Face God. Fall at his feet and trust his wisdom. Oswald Chambers gives the same advice: "We have to pray with our eyes on God, not on the difficulties."[2]

Several times in Moses's story, after Israel had sinned, he said something similar to this: "You have sinned a great sin. And now I will go up to the LORD; perhaps I can make atonement for your sin" (Exod. 32:30). Sin is this world's biggest problem. Even though Moses is depicted as a savior of Israel, Christ the anointed sacrificial lamb would truly liberate men from this awful slavery, reconcile them to God, and take away the sin of the world (John 1:29). Jesus, the true atonement for sin, makes men "at-one-ment" with God.

Intercessory prayer has staggering power. Those prayers have mileage and go places we cannot; as we trust and keep our eyes on God, we cry out for him to move people with distanced hearts back to Christ, the perfect atonement.

In the Trenches with Jesus: His parents named him Simon, meaning one "that hears, that obeys." When Jesus chose him as an apostle, he renamed him Peter, meaning "stone." Before Jesus's crucifixion, in an intimate moment, Jesus reverted to this disciple's given name and said, "Simon, Simon, behold, Satan demanded to have you, that he might sift you like wheat, but I have prayed for you that your faith may not fail. And when you have turned again, strengthen your brothers" (Luke 22:31–32). In reply, Peter vowed, "Lord, I am ready to go with you both to prison and to death." The Lord understood Peter's good intentions, but he also knew that under pressure, the talons of the devil sink deep. Jesus predicted what would happen before dawn and the crowing of roosters: "You will deny me three times."

Have you, like Jesus, ever cautioned a child of God with a warning and a promise of prayer? What a beautiful combination—worthy of contemplation and practice.

> Trust in God. We can only see a little bit down the road, but God can see around every curve.
>
> Taste and see that the LORD is good; blessed is the one who takes refuge in him. —Psalm 34:8 NIV
>
> "God bless us, every one!" —Tiny Tim in *A Christmas Carol*, Charles Dickens

My Dog Tag

"And the Lord's servant, _____, must not be quarrelsome but kind to everyone, able to teach, patiently enduring evil, correcting [her] opponents with

gentleness. God may perhaps grant them repentance leading to a knowledge of the truth" (2 Tim. 2:24–25).

In the Trenches with Cathy: When I was eleven, my mom made
me a bathing suit, a modest one that didn't even compare to a
yellow polka-dot bikini. However, Mom made one error. When
looking for fabric, she shopped in the terry cloth department.
I'm not talking the cheap, threadbare, made-in-China fabric.
No! She chose a five-star, hotel-quality piece that could double
as carpet.

She sewed a pale blue, one-piece, super absorbent, maxi
pad-type swimsuit. When I tried it on, I looked a bit roly-poly. I
hadn't lost my baby fat, and the fabric nap added inches to my
girth. When girls' day "only" arrived, and my younger sister and
I walked to the pool, I determined to get in the deep end. Even
though I didn't know how to swim, I was tired of splashing in
the shallow kiddie end. From midway poolside, I shoved off and
made it to water that was about six feet deep. There, I discovered my feet couldn't touch the bottom. My terry cloth swimsuit
immediately slurped up gallons of water, and I sank like a bag of
potatoes.

Meanwhile, my stick-thin sister clung to the pool ladder, her
terry cloth suit flattened against her body. She simply looked
like an adorable wet kitten. She was safe. She had no idea of my
predicament. My toes eventually touched the bottom, and I toe-
bounced to the surface, gasped for air, went under again, and
toe-bounced up again. Sink. Rise up. Gasp for air. Sink. Rise up.
Gasp for air. I was too panicked to ask for help.

If I had found my voice and screamed for help, others
would have come to my rescue. The lifeguard was perched near

me. Women and girls of all ages were within spitting distance. I recognize that God enabled me to toe-bounce enough times to propel me to the side, out of danger from my foolish choice.

Plenty of women splashed in the shallow end of the pool, while I almost drowned. I fear that our everyday cares may blind us to when another woman near us is sinking, sinking, sinking. She may be overwhelmed by life, needing our rescue through a hand up and intercessory prayers. She might be inching under to temptations, needing a warning and a prayer much like Jesus offered Peter. Be your sister's lifeguard. Pay attention. Talk to your Father often about the women within your circle of care. Throw out the lifeline. Rescue the perishing.

God loves you and Moses equally, and your intercessory prayer will cause God to respond within his wisdom to care for your family, friends, enemies, and the lost. Pray. Intercede for others.

Combat Mission for This Week
Each day, intercede for unbelievers and Christians.

Historical Field Guide

John Wesley wrote what has become known as the Covenant Prayer. In London, at a gathering of eighteen hundred people at a French church on Monday, August 11, 1755, Wesley asked attendees to make personal vows at what he called a covenant service.

Today, those willing to pray the Covenant Prayer will discover rather quickly if they are withholding any part of their lives from our generous Lord. Certain phrases may be challenging to pray depending upon individual circumstances. One young woman prays this prayer in her closet on her knees each day. The prayer sets the bar high, and the vows call each person to a humble commitment to trust that God knows what is best for each child of his. The version below arrives through the Book of Offices of the British Methodist Church, 1936. Copy the prayer in your handwriting and place it where you can see it and pray it often. Through this exercise, discover your own weaknesses and our Father's abundant graces.

Covenant Prayer

I am no longer my own, but thine.
Put me to what thou wilt, rank me with whom thou wilt.
Put me to doing, put me to suffering.
Let me be employed for thee or laid aside for thee,
exalted for thee or brought low for thee.
Let me be full, let me be empty.
Let me have all things, let me have nothing.
I freely and heartily yield all things to thy pleasure and disposal.
And now, O glorious and blessed God, Father, Son and Holy Spirit,
thou art mine, and I am thine.
So be it.
And the covenant which I have made on earth,
let it be ratified in heaven.
Amen.[3]

My Combat Prayer
O God, allow the things that break your heart to break mine.

O Jerusalem, Jerusalem, the city that kills the prophets and stones those who are sent to it! How often would I have gathered your children together as a hen gathers her brood under her wings, and you were not willing! (Matt. 23:37).

Tactical Training

1. Read Exodus 4:10–17. When Moses considered only himself, minus God's abilities, he was at first reluctant to obey God's call. Has any time in your prayer journey mirrored his reluctance and/or his eventual obedience? Describe God's character revealed in these verses.

2. Read Exodus 32:7–10, 11–13, and 30–35. Have you interceded for a "stiff-necked" person (arrogant, haughty, and unresponsive)? Have you trusted God and remained steady in your intercessory prayers? What impressed you in these verses?

3. Read Exodus 32:30 and Ephesians 2:13–18. Within Moses's story and the old law, the word atonement occurs. In Leviticus 16:30, what does the word atonement mean? What was the atonement covering in the temple? What did it represent?

4. Read Deuteronomy 34:7 to find how God sustained Moses to the very end. Women experience loss of sleep and weariness some days; how does God sustain you? List the refreshments you receive from God to aid your daily walk or your prayers for family and others.

5. Read what Jesus said to Simon in Luke 22:31–32. When have you followed this lead of Jesus and cautioned a child of God with a warning plus a promise of prayer? What were the results?

6. Read Numbers 12:3 about Moses's humility and Psalm 25:9. How do humility and prayer complement each other?

7. Have you interceded for one of God's own that strayed? Such prayers might include phrases such as, "Jesus, let them hit rock bottom and turn to you," or "Father, let them come to the end of themselves and see you." Share your similar prayers.

8. Has God convicted you to pray for your enemies and those without Christ? Pray now. Has he alerted your heart about a specific person who would benefit from your intercessory prayer? Pray now. Continue these prayers throughout the week.

My Diary from the Trenches

Expect God to lay concerns for his people on your heart.
Respond in on-the-spot prayer. Record your victories.

Chapter Seven

Divine Intervention During Heart-Wrenching Times

Hezekiah

"The LORD has heard my plea; the LORD accepts my prayer."
—Psalm 6:9

"It's cancer."

"I don't love you."

"The company is downsizing."

"I don't believe in God anymore."

"We can't find a heartbeat."

These gut-wrenching moments shatter our worlds, crush our hearts, and wring us out. The only place for a woman who wants to win those battles is on her face at the feet of her Savior. The goal from this place is survival and relief from the debilitating pressure of pain. But the real cry of a woman's heart is "No!" She wants to sidestep the trouble. She wants God to step in and change her story. She wants God's divine intervention. Women's stories often change, but sometimes they don't. With confidence, a winning woman will embrace this truth: God provides what she needs even when the answer is not what she wants.

"Beloved, do not be surprised at the fiery trial when it comes upon you to test you, as though something strange were happening to you" (1 Pet. 4:12). Peter assures us in this verse that trials happen and they serve a purpose. No one welcomes hard times, and we are almost always shocked when they occur. To soften the blow of sudden bad news, we can prepare now for what we will do. Beverly Ross, Christian speaker and counselor, says, "Prepare in the light for what you will do in the dark." Beverly has experienced hard times, and she knows the reality is not *if* hard times come. Hard times happen. Bad things do happen to good people.

Hezekiah's Story

At the age of twenty-five, Hezekiah became king of Judah and he reigned twenty-nine years. His father Ahaz left a legacy of horrendous idolatry. King Ahaz closed the temple of God, built altars in every corner of Jerusalem to false gods of the pagan nations, and even sacrificed some of his children by throwing them into fire as worship to an idol. In Hezekiah's childhood, he lost siblings to a fire at his father's command, and surely the fear of *Am I next?* haunted his sleep.

Yet, despite his over-the-top dysfunctional father, Hezekiah chose a different path for his life and kingship. He would not sacrifice his children to a stone or wooden idol. In the first month of his reign, he reopened the temple and tore down all evidence of idol worship. "He trusted in the LORD, the God of Israel, so that there was none like him among all the kings of Judah after him, nor among those who were before him." The Scriptures further testify about him, "For he held fast to the Lord. He did not depart from following him, but kept the commandments that the Lord commanded Moses" (2 Kings 18:5–6). And the best news was "the Lord was with him; wherever he went out, he prospered" (7).

Life in Judah was good for the first fourteen years of Hezekiah's reign, and then the Assyrians invaded. The Assyrians, just a few years before, conquered Israel, the country just north of Judah, and now they were at Jerusalem's walls threatening to do the same. King Hezekiah had expected the attack, strengthened the walls, rerouted the city's water supply, and increased their weapons supply. After completing those projects, he held a town meeting and said, "Be strong and courageous. Do not be afraid or dismayed before the king of Assyria and all the horde that is with him, for there are more with us than with him." King Hezekiah confirmed the Assyrians had only brute strength on their side, while the Judeans had God as chief of their ranks. "With him is an arm of flesh, but with us is the Lord our God, to help us and to fight our battles" (2 Chron. 32:7–8).

Prepared, the residents of Jerusalem waited. What would the Assyrians do? Surely God would not let them invade. Surely they would just go home and leave Jerusalem alone. But their eyes and ears soon told a very different story. The Assyrians surrounded Jerusalem, and their leader, Sennacherib, began the greatest battle, the battle of psychological warfare. He yelled taunts and offered false peace. He urged the citizens of Jerusalem to surrender. He boasted of all his previous victories. He advised them that Hezekiah was misleading them, but his most obnoxious gibe was a lie: that God would not save them, and he classified the God of the universe with the idols of man.

King Hezekiah instructed his people not to answer the jeering—the mind games had begun. Nowhere to run. Nowhere to hide. It didn't just *look* hopeless; by man's standards, it *was* hopeless. They could not fight this army—that would be suicide and they could not outlast them. From this place of utter helplessness and desperation, Hezekiah cried out to God for immediate intervention.

> O LORD, the God of Israel, enthroned above the cherubim, you are the God, you alone, of all the kingdoms of the earth; you have made heaven and earth. Incline your ear, O LORD, and hear; open your eyes, O LORD, and see; and hear the words of Sennacherib, which he has sent to mock the living God. Truly, O LORD, the kings of Assyria have laid waste the nations and their lands . . . . O LORD our God, save us, please, from his hand, that all the kingdoms of the earth may know that you, O LORD, are God alone. (2 Kings 19:15–19)

King Hezekiah boldly approached God and asked him to act. And God did. The next morning the city of Jerusalem awoke to an eerie quiet. The noise outside the walls was gone. The bedlam of the enemy army was silent. The citizens discovered that an angel of God had struck down 185,000 enemies in a single night. The army of Judah did not lift one piece of weaponry—by divine intervention the victory was won.

When It Looks Hopeless—the Gift of Grace

Tears streak down the face of a woman in pain. She cries, but what is she to do? The enemy of her soul offers dim options: worry, anger, fear, offense, hate, depression, and despair, to name only a few. None of these bring any comfort, peace, or hope. Only God can bring light into her pain and uncertainty. When troubles flood her life, the woman who wants to win the battle will look up. When a woman stands in rising water and fears drowning, she will focus on her Savior who treads on stormy waves.

God's Word does not guarantee that she will always get her preferred way, but it does promise that God will never leave her. Those who long to win against wickedness stand upon the Rock, Jesus Christ, to avoid the undertow of evil. Scripture promises peace that makes no sense, light in the darkest valleys, direction when obscurity seems prevalent, and hope when all looks bleak. All hope of rescue is found in Jesus. He steps in, this Prince of Peace, Light, and Way. As clutching hands cling to his faithful hands, he guides us through all valleys, even the shadow of death. He alone can walk us to green pastures and beside calm waters.

The unimaginable becomes manageable. The impossible becomes possible. The heartbreak becomes bearable. All this and more done by the power of grace. Because Christ lives in us, "we have all received, grace upon grace" (John 1:16). Grace is the divine power which equips women to live godly lives. God's grace includes all his good gifts, his mercy, and his salvation.

God always initiates grace, and because of grace, lives aren't limited by human potential or limited resources. Grace, a precious gift, empowered by the Holy Spirit, gives us everything we need for life and godliness. Max Lucado tweeted, "Grace is simply another word for God's tumbling, rumbling reservoir of God's strength and protection."[1]

Grace pulls us through, lifts us up, equips us to stand and eventually overcome.

Praiseworthy Promises for Pressing Problems

Scriptural promises give assurance, confirm God's power, and affirm eventual victory. The following ten are found in Psalms, a few of the nuggets of truth that encourage and equip.

- God is my strength (18:1).
- In God's presence is fullness of joy (16:11).
- When I call, God answers (17:6).
- He restores my soul (23:3).
- Whom shall I fear? The Lord is my stronghold (27:1).
- He turns my mourning into dancing (30:11).
- My times are in God's hands (31:15).
- God is my help and shield (33:20).
- The Lord is near to the brokenhearted (34:18).
- Delight in the Lord and he will give you the desires of your heart (37:4).

These promises are simply the appetizer of the full-meal-plus-dessert promises tucked throughout God's Word. Open your Bible and feast on his goodness, provision, and grace. You will leave full and overflowing, satisfied by his love and faithfulness. And once you've tasted, you will hunger for more.

Armor of God

Sword: "You equipped _____ with strength for the battle" (Ps. 18:39).

Shield: "And my God will supply every need of _____ according to his riches in glory in Christ Jesus" (Phil. 4:19).

Shoes: "_____, draw near to God, and he will draw near to you" (James 4:8).

In the Trenches with Deanna: The day began rough. I was with my mom and dad at her first appointment with a radiologist, the final step in this cancer battle. My phone was on silent and buried in my purse, but I could feel it vibrating again and again. I was frustrated. I did not want to be disturbed. My mom needed my complete attention, but when the doctor walked out of the room for a minute, I quickly checked my phone. I had a dozen or more missed calls—several from my cowboy, a few from our employee, and more from our neighbor. As I was scrolling, my phone began to vibrate again. At my mom's prompting, I answered. At an alarming speed, my neighbor gushed words at me: my cowboy was hurt . . . on his way to the hospital . . . couldn't walk . . . lots of blood . . . severe pain . . . she had my kids.

Panic engulfed me. Tears flowed before I even disconnected the call. My parents propelled my frozen, shocked self out the door and assured me they would be right behind me.

The thirty-minute drive felt like a lifetime. I cried and babbled inconsolably to God. The shock and unknown threatened to drown me in fear-filled waters. My prayers were a jumbled mess with a common thread, "Just let him be okay!" I'm not sure how I got to the ER since the journey was a complete blur. Thank God for his mercies.

Once the car was parked, I ran. The nurses were waiting for me and took me straight back to him. As I barged through the door, the sight that greeted me was far from what I expected. The doctor, a friend of ours, was laughing and joking as he cut my cowboy's jeans off. They were even arguing about his boots. My cowboy did not want those cut off. He said, "Just pull them off." The only real drama of the scene was the blood. When Dr.

Dan saw my confusion, he quickly explained the important job the morphine was doing.

While Dr. Dan steadily worked, I got the full story. While riding, a horse had reared up and fallen on my cowboy, and he had been pinned under the horse and saddle. If the horse had immediately jumped up after his fall, he then would have stepped on my husband's head. Thankfully, by the grace of God, the horse remained still as my horse whisperer calmly talked to the animal and waited for someone to find them. My young son was the first on the scene, and he ran and grabbed our employee, and they pulled my cowboy from under the eighteen hundred-pound horse. They kept pressure on his wound, loaded him in a pickup, and drove him to the emergency room.

The horse's hind foot had ripped open his leg near the main artery. Dr. Dan carefully cleaned the wound, sent my cowboy for scans, and then sewed him up. The tests revealed no breaks or major damage. Later Dr. Dan told my cowboy how close he had come to training horses in heaven. If the fully exposed artery had torn, my cowboy would have bled out before help arrived.

A little time to mend, and my cowboy was back on horses after just three months. The miracle of the whole rodeo-gone-bad still staggers me. I am beyond thankful God heard my desperate cries and others' pleas for his gracious intervention.

In the Trenches with Jesus: During Jesus's ministry on earth, he provided immediate intervention for countless people. He healed, cast out demons, raised the dead, brought peace, forgave sins, and provided physical nourishment. According to John, the beloved disciple, many things Jesus did are not recorded, "Were every one of them to be written, I suppose that the world itself could not contain the books" (John 21:25). Jesus answered the desperate prayers of more people during his ministry than we could possibly imagine, and he was their deliverance in more ways than they realized.

During Jesus's most desperate hour, he too cried out for divine intervention. He did not want to endure what his future held. "He fell on his face and prayed, saying, 'My Father, if it be possible, let this cup pass from me'" (Matt. 26:39). Jesus's anguished plea to his father mirrors our cries when we want life to go a different, easier, less painful route. Jesus knew the physical and emotional trauma that lay before him, and he wanted God to provide a different way. The ending of Jesus's impassioned supplication depicts a life and heart fully devoted and fully trusting. "Not as I will, but as you will" (Matt. 26:39). Jesus entrusted the circumstances and his very life into the hands of the Father who loved him.

Jesus's humble obedience, which led to his death, also led him to his resurrection and our ultimate intervention. He died so we could live—the greatest divine intervention we will ever receive.

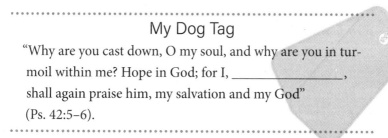

My Dog Tag

"Why are you cast down, O my soul, and why are you in turmoil within me? Hope in God; for I, _____, shall again praise him, my salvation and my God" (Ps. 42:5–6).

When God Says No

No exact ratio exists, but because you are a woman of prayer, at some time you have received a no from God. We typically want our way during a crisis, and no is not an easy word to hear. In hopes of swaying the outcome, we may logically explain to God why he should say yes. God knows how to answer each request in perfection, and all our rationalizations will not change God's perfect answers.

A few things to consider when *during* prayers do not produce our desired results: What is the motive? "When you ask, you do not receive, because you ask with wrong motives" (James 4:3 NIV). Is pride driving the request? "God opposes the proud but shows favor to the humble" (James 4:6 NIV). Have your prayers been persistent? Jesus tells the parable of the tenacious widow to show the importance of not giving up in prayer (Luke 18:1–8). Are the prayers lifted up in faith? "According to your faith be it done to you" (Matt. 9:29). Another possibility: Is God asking you to wait? Maybe the answer isn't *no* but *not yet*—"Wait for the Lord; be strong and take heart and wait for the Lord" (Ps. 27:14 NIV).

If all of these seem to be in line with God's Word and yet the desired answer is still not given, then winning women can still remain steadfast believing the following Scriptures:

- "'For my thoughts are not your thoughts, neither are your ways my ways,' declares the Lord. 'For as the heavens are higher than the earth, so are my ways higher than your ways and my thoughts than your thoughts'" (Isa. 55:8–9).
- "His divine power has given us everything we need for a godly life through our knowledge of him who called us by his own glory and goodness" (2 Pet. 1:3 NIV).
- "We know that for those who love God all things work together for good" (Rom. 8:28).

- "Oh give thanks to the LORD, for he is good, for his stead-fast love endures forever!" (Ps. 107:1).

Understanding may never come when God denies the cry of our heart because his ways outdistance ours, but we always know that he can bring good out of our pain if we let him. These truths anchor us in God and keep us moored during our storms.

In the Trenches with Cathy: When our first child, Russell, was two, I talked to my husband about having a second baby. We settled on a time frame and the Lord brought Sheryle into our family. When our children were seven and four, I considered having a third baby, but a third child wasn't on my husband's radar. By then, we both had made the habit of inquiring of God whether our plans were his plans. Apparently, God was telling my husband no, but I still had thoughts of that third baby.

As I age, I look back on God's decisive no to having more children, and I thank him. He brought many people into my life, and I had the energy to take care of the extra people. During the time I wanted a third child, I was working full-time in our family business, and our children went along to our job sites. We also babysat a boy for a single-again mom. Within another four years, my husband's grandmother, a ninety-year-old who lived next door, needed near-constant attention due to the onset of senility. With the most flexible schedule in our family, we looked after her and cooked meals four days a week. By then, the Lord had me teaching women's classes and our children were teenagers, and we had extra teens in our home for meals and fun. One girl lived with us for a while.

Shortly after that stage of life, we had an elderly neighbor near one hundred who had a single daughter who never married and didn't drive, and I assisted their main caregiver. Overlapping, we also babysat a single mom's infant. By the time our children married, I was writing an inspirational newspaper column, and we had four parents who were in light stages of needing help, and five beautiful grandchildren arrived in those years. My mother, in a slow, debilitating decline, was bedridden for six years, some in her home and some at a skilled nursing facility. Dad and I were her caregivers for the duration, and I was cooking *take-in* food for my in-laws. Three months after my mother died, both my in-laws fell on the same night. And the cycle started over.

I don't write about giving care to others for applause but rather to acknowledge God's long-distance vision, of him seeing what I could not see—the future. And by his grace, all those people lived near us, and I didn't travel to another state to help my family.

I now know that God saw my future, and while we would have loved a third child, I still embrace God's *no.* Through his foreknowledge, he allowed me rest, gave me energy, and enabled me to stay somewhat sane. I remain grateful. At this writing, I'm still employed full-time with my husband's company, but we work from our home base where my flexible schedule allows me to assist in caregiving for my dad. Our children and families now live on the same acreage with us, and my dad is within a few miles.

We are the Waltons. We are blessed. And God arranged it all when he said *no* to one prayer request.

Combat Mission for This Week
Lay your requests before God, trusting him with the timing and answers.

─────────── Historical Field Guide ───────────

"The history of the church may almost be said to be a history of the trials and sufferings of its members, as experienced at the hands of wicked men."[2] This first line in *Foxe's Book of Martyrs* portrays martyrs throughout Christian history, and according to Amazon's editorial the book takes about thirteen hours to read. It's a telling amount of time that says a staggering number of men, women, and children suffered and died for the name of Christ. They held tight to their hope in God but still traveled the path that led to their deaths. Surely they cried out for divine intervention. Surely at least some desperately wanted to live. And yet God, in his infinite wisdom, allowed them to die for their beliefs. Grace gave them courage to stand firm, and grace allowed them to die for their faith. Not delivered from the suffering of this earth, instead they were delivered into eternity, to their reward—a tangible example of when God says no for a better yes.

Christian martyrs have embraced these truths: "Be faithful unto death, and I will give you the crown of life" (Rev. 2:10); "For they loved not their lives even unto death" (Rev. 12:11); and "Precious in the sight of the LORD is the death of his saints" (Ps. 116:15).

My Combat Prayer

Hear my prayer, O Lord; in your faithfulness answer.

Hear my prayer, O LORD; give ear to my pleas for mercy!
In your faithfulness answer me, in your righteousness!
(Ps. 143:1).

Tactical Training

1. We all have messy, hard, wrenching lives at times. What was the cry of your heart during those times? What was God's response? How has that experience changed your walk with God?

2. Consider how God equips us: 2 Timothy 3:16–17, Hebrews 13:20–21, and Ephesians 4:11–12. What are you doing now to prepare for those hard places? Are you "battle ready"?

3. In the Old Testament, what men or women cried out for God in difficult times? List God's response and the outcome. Which of these stories from God's Word most encourages you?

4. When life gets hard, unhealthy habits lead even winning women to worry. Read Matthew 6:25–34. Do you worry first or pray first? When worry surfaces, turn the thought into a prayer and give God your worries.

5. Read Romans 8:28. Have you seen the fulfilment of this verse in your life? Are you still waiting for a good outcome? If you are waiting in faith for a better outcome, consider Hebrews 11 and the women who never saw fulfilled promises during their lifetimes but still trusted God.

6. Are you good at waiting, or is your patience thin? If you have ever walked by faith, you have "waited" on God. What typically happens when you wait? Do you complain or try to take things into your own hands? Do any of those things help? How should we wait? Read Lamentations 3:26.

7. In Luke 18, Jesus tells the parable of the persistent widow, urging us not to give up or lose heart because prayer not only changes situations but also changes our hearts. Have you stopped praying for something? Are you willing to follow the widow's example and practice persistence, trusting our good God with the end results?

8. King David, as a direct result of his sin, faces a heart-wrenching situation in 2 Samuel 12. His son from Bathsheba is dying. He puts on sackcloth and ashes and cries out to the Lord, begging for the life of his son, but God does not change his mind. The child dies. Read the story and consider David's end response to the will of God. Does this make sense to you? Can you rest and find peace even when your will and God's will don't match? Are you okay with living in God's will and not your own?

My Diary from the Trenches

Expect God's presence this week and be alert for his divine intervention. Give thanks and record your victories.

Chapter Eight

Seeking Direction During Suffering

Hagar

> "The LORD looks down from heaven on the children of man, to see if there are any who understand, who seek after God." — Psalm 14:2

How do you respond when you find yourself dealing with suffering? Most women seek a way out of suffering, and those who are trapped in misery may long for or dream about freedom from the cruelties they endure. Generally, women seek a roadmap back into a settled, pleasant, or at least tolerable life. The young servant of Sarai, Hagar, faced an intolerable situation, and she eventually learned what we can also know: God sees, God knows, and God comforts.

Hagar's Dilemmas

Imagine Hagar's early life.

Her homeland was Egypt, and because of poverty, family debts, or lack of family, this young girl was up for sale. A transaction took place and people who spoke a different language whisked her away. More frightened than she'd ever been, she joined a large caravan of people and animals, who had an elderly man as master. Day by day, Hagar began to grasp their language and what was expected of her. Soon she began to help the mistress, Sarai, who remained beautiful despite her advancing years.

Hagar expected they might travel to a city that her wealthy master owned, but that hope dimmed. They had no permanent dwellings. They were nomads with a compound of tents and several hundred fighting men, trained to protect them and the massive herds.

She had learned early in life that a servant's place was lonely even in a crowd of people, and her best strategy was to do her work, remain silent, and go unnoticed. She kept her head bowed. Her eyes averted. She followed orders. Her life of drudgery had no freedoms. Hagar had no voice in what happened to her and no monetary means to relieve her bondage. She was trapped.

As she passed puberty, she began to get subtle hints from her barren mistress that perhaps Hagar might birth a child for her master. She had no choice. She then did as commanded and lived a dual life as slave to her mistress and wife to her aged master, knowing if a child was born she would only become a surrogate mother because her baby would belong to Sarai.

We don't know Hagar's thoughts, but servants often suffered oppression. They endured strict circumstances and were punished for the slightest infractions, often harshly with whip pings and beatings. She lived in a barbaric age of history when marauding bands took girls captive from other clans as brides. Rulers had the most beautiful women in the land captured to take into their harems. The tribes of the earth had not settled into the common civilities of the free world today.

One example of the cultural mindset toward women is in Judges 5. In song lyrics, a Queen Mother's maidens comfort her by suggesting the army was delayed because they were divvying up war loot: "Have they not found and divided the spoil?—A womb or two for every man" (Judg. 5:30). The captive females were referred to as simply "wombs" to supply heirs. For women living in that era, another difficult custom existed: for a man to have one, two, or more wives.

Hagar could only expect shelter and food. She had no grand dreams of freedom, family, or pleasure. She was forced to leave everything she knew in Egypt.

Armor of God

Sword: "Send out your light and your truth; let them lead _____; let them bring _____to your holy hill and to your dwelling!" (Ps. 43:3).

Shield: "As for you, O LORD, you will not restrain your mercy from _____; your steadfast love and your faithfulness will ever preserve _____!" (Ps. 40:11).

Shoes: "The steps of _____ are established by the LORD, when he delights in _____'s way" (Ps. 37:23).

Blessings in the Wilderness

Hagar became part of the contradiction in Abram and Sarai's lives. Latayne C. Scott in *The Hinge of Your History: The Phases of Faith* mentions a recurring pattern in the Bible and in our lives: promise, contradiction, and resolution.[1] Abram and Sarai's lives settled into years without the promised heir—the contradiction—between the promise and resolution. We know nothing of Sarai's angst in placing Hagar in her husband's arms, but she convinced Abram to take Hagar as a second wife.

After Hagar conceived by Abram, the *New International Version* says she began to "despise her mistress" (Gen. 16:4). Most commentators agree that the wording in the NIV does not reflect the original Hebrew, which implies one of the women thought less of herself, not naming which one. Certainly, Sarai could have been crushed by the knowledge that the inability to have a child now rested upon her. Hagar might have become haughty, because great turmoil occurs when a maidservant "displaces her mistress" (Prov. 30:23). Common sense dictates that anytime two women share a husband, the reality exists for a volcanic eruption. The tension between pregnant Hagar and barren Sarai must have been palpable.

Sarai blamed Abram and told him to fix the problem, and Genesis 16:5 literally reads, "You are responsible for my violence." Again, the original Hebrew isn't clear whether Sarai or Hagar committed the violence. During messiness do we try to shift blame? Do we hold grudges against others instead of searching our hearts for wrong attitudes or blatant sins? Abram stepped back from the women's squabble, and he told Sarai, "'Do with her whatever you think best.' Then Sarai mistreated Hagar; so she fled from her" (Gen. 16:6 NIV).

Hagar chose to run to a desert rather than endure further persecution. Sometimes that is the only answer when women face abuse. But don't we do that in lesser circumstances, too?

We want escape from problems? We ignore them. We pretend they don't exist through doing nothing, but we know messy lives aren't straightened by skedaddling from minor problems.

Oppressed, Hagar fled to a spring in the desert, but God in his mercy was about to direct her. The angel of the Lord found her there and said, "Hagar, servant of Sarai, where have you come from and where are you going?" (Gen. 16:8). God, with exactness and compassion, called her by name, identified her station in life, and asked, "Where have you come from and where are you going?"—two poignant questions, relevant to all women. She admitted to running away from Sarai, and the Lord told her to return and submit, and God promised, "I will so increase your descendants they will be too numerous to count." He confirmed her pregnancy and that she would bear a son, and the original Hebrew said he would live among his people or to the east of his people.

"So she called the name of the Lord who spoke to her, 'You are a God of seeing,' for she said, 'Truly here I have seen him who looks after me'" (Gen 16:13). Hagar went back to the encampment and in due time gave birth to Ishmael. She is the first recorded woman since Eve to "see" God and receive personal direction. Personal encounters with God provide women with life maneuvers, because his instructions are clear and direct.

God continued to direct Abram and Sarai and changed their names to Abraham and Sarah. Later, when the son of promise, Isaac, arrived and was weaned, Abraham hosted a celebration. But when Sarah caught the young teen Ishmael teasing Isaac, Sarah wanted Ishmael gone, so the heavy hearted Abraham sent Hagar and Ishmael away with only a few provisions (Gen. 21:8–20).

Again Hagar finds herself in a desert place, and she is desperate for water to survive their immediate troubles and direction for their uncertain future. She places Ishmael (whose name means "God hears") under the shade of a desert bush and moves a short distance away, for she cannot bear to watch her only son die. Ishmael moans with thirst and Hagar receives a message: "God has heard the voice of the boy where he is" (Gen. 21:17), meaning God has responded positively to someone's prayer. No one appeared to her, but she heard a voice from heaven directing her not to fear and showing her a well of water where she filled a wineskin and gave her son a drink.

My Dog Tag

"_____, if you receive my words and treasure up my commandments with you, making your ear attentive to wisdom and inclining your heart to understanding; yes, if you call out for insight and raise your voice for understanding . . . then you will understand the fear of the Lord and find the knowledge of God" (Prov. 2:1–5).

In the Trenches with Deanna: While in the third grade, my son became a competitive gymnast. This happened overnight. One day he was playing baseball, and the next he was flipping through the air. This caused a major upset in our home. His practice took a crazy amount of hours, and the gym was over an hour away. The only logical step was to homeschool him, one of those things I promised *never* to do. I had no idea where to begin.

Thankfully, God surrounded me on every side with godly women who had already homeschooled. They offered advice and resources, and the amazing part was how their counsel matched. God confirmed his direction multiple times through these women. Brady, my tumbling and flying gymnast, easily adjusted to homeschool and we were on our way.

I mistakenly thought the direction about homeschooling was over. God led, I had followed, the end—but God was not done. Brooke, my then-first grader who thought she was an adult, was experiencing some rough patches. Her strong will seemed to be growing before my eyes. Our relationship consisted of fights, tears, and continual frustration. As I sought to uncover the source of this problem, I began to spend time in her classroom at school. The root of the problem became glaringly obvious. My strong-willed child was also a charmer and her actions resulted in her getting her way. After trying multiple ways to correct the problem, it became clear we needed drastic change, but again, I had no idea what that change should be.

Seeking direction regarding Brooke, the same advice was given: "You should homeschool her." I looked for different advice. I could not imagine being a full-time teacher to this teacher's pet. No other advice surfaced, so I stalled.

As a surprise one day, I grabbed McDonald's fast food for Brooke's school lunch. However, I was over thirty minutes early, so I waited outside her classroom and watched. What I saw broke my heart. This headstrong child was putting on a show for her class while her teacher worked with other students. I could see the teacher was annoyed but allowed the antics. I withdrew Brooke the next day. Finally, after almost a complete school year, I gave in to God's direction. My resistance cost us valuable time, but God faithfully continues to lead us in this homeschool journey, and now I have a precious relationship with my young teenage daughter. Would I have chosen this path for my family? No. But now I am thankful God led us to homeschooling.

His ways are higher and without a doubt they are best.

In the Trenches with Jesus: Mark writes about the beginning of Jesus's ministry, "The Spirit immediately drove him out into the wilderness. And he was in the wilderness forty days, being tempted by Satan. And he was with the wild animals, and the angels were ministering to him" (1:12–13). Imagine a place barren of trees or shelter, and consider the mix of setting and characters mentioned: Jesus, the Spirit of God, angels, Satan, and a barren desert inhabited by wild animals. The physical difficulties of living in a place devoid of food and water with wild animals for forty days would prove daunting, but add in Satan and temptations, and the portrait of Jesus's forty days in a barren place seems completely oppressive and dark. However, remember the presence of holiness in that wilderness.

Consider the forces of good that are present in the desert: Jesus (holiness in the tent of an earthly body), the Spirit (comforter and guide), and angels (messengers sent to aid believers). A powerful host of heaven joined forces to support Jesus, who was the willing sacrificial lamb, to assist him to win the battle in that landscape of evil.

Dear conquering woman, Jesus was led by the Spirit into the desert, but his Father didn't leave him there. Sometimes we are sent into a desert, sometimes we stumble into a desert, sometimes we willfully walk into a desert, but our Father will not abandon our hearts in that place. He will speak grace to us there and lead us out. Look for him when you find yourself in a wilderness without answers, in a place that has no visible way out, in a place where you "feel" deserted—pray and expect the army of heaven to assist and revive you: Jesus, the Holy Spirit, and angels. Remember the mix of evil and holy with Jesus in the desert. Remember who won.

Pray and be not afraid, for evil is no match for the Lion of Judah, the victor in all things.

In the Trenches with Cathy: When I needed direction, my heart-wrenching struggles in prayer occurred in the early hours after midnight. Late-night hours are some of the best times for prayer during crises because the phone isn't ringing. Visitors aren't knocking on the door. No one clamors for attention, and most people in my time zone are asleep . . . except for God.

We had a marriage crisis at one time, and I was in turmoil. I had young children, meals to cook, a business to run, and laundry to do during the day. Time alone was rare, and I was frantic for direction. The only time I could really pour out my heart to God was at night. We lived in the country (still do), and I especially remember one night near one o'clock that I got out of bed and walked outside in the moonlight and passionately prayed for direction and God's intervention. No immediate answer surfaced, but a gradual understanding took place over the next few months, and my husband and I settled upon a mutual path.

On another occasion, after receiving bad news that could result in death or not, I spent a night on my knees seeking God's path. Because of the quiet hours, I could beg, weep, and plead in private, and after some months, that crisis passed. While severe problems, physical or spiritual, can cause crises, they can also drive us to deep and purposeful prayer.

"Dark Night of the Soul" (in Spanish: *La noche oscura del alma*) is the title of a poem written by sixteenth-century Spanish poet and Roman Catholic Saint John of the Cross. The poem details in two parts the struggles of a soul to connect with God. F. Scott Fitzgerald said, "In a real dark night of the soul it is always three o'clock in the morning."

Because of unbearable pain, those *during* midnight prayers are often the ones we remember with clarity. As I look back on outcomes, I recognize God's presence and determine without a doubt that God answered, directed, and eventually relieved my agony.

Hagar's Blessings

God directed and mapped out Hagar's future to give her multiple blessings:

- She has a clear picture from God that she and Ishmael will have a future.
- Even though cast out, she is finally free.
- She no longer serves a mistress or is a second wife in Abraham's household.
- Her beloved Ishmael belongs to her and is not reckoned as Sarai's child.
- She has received a promise from God of having her own huge family.

Whew! In a moment of seeming disaster in being cast out, Hagar's life dramatically changes, and she learns that her life and Ishmael's life will not end in a barren desert. She will survive and thrive.

Matthew Henry commented about Hagar, "God brings us into a wilderness, and there meets us."[2] The prophet Hosea recorded that Israel, because of her sin, also landed in a wilderness, and God said, "Therefore, behold, I will allure her, and bring her into the wilderness, and speak tenderly to her" (Hosea 2:14).

Have you experienced God's tender mercies in that way, in a desert place where there was no other hope of refreshment? When you were thirsty for direction, hungry for answers, or alone in contradictions, did God meet you and direct your heart? Perhaps you received a simple reminder to turn to him, or you may have received a literal path to take. Our most lonely and dark times can occur after the sun goes down and family and friends retire for the night and we feel alone with our problems and thoughts. Turn to your Father, the Night Watchman, for he specializes in directing the weary.

Alone in the Dark Night of the Soul

Winning women, if you find yourself alone in the night seeking direction, you have at least three options: prayer, Bible study, and seeking wise counsel.

First, seek God in prayer: God, fully present every twenty-four hours, can direct, comfort, and grant rest. If we allow our minds to fill with ungodly thoughts, regrets, and wrongs, if we give in to negative thinking, we may sink into despair and hopelessness—that our problems are too massive even for God to handle. Choose to seek God's solutions and comfort.

Several of L. M. Montgomery's novels feature Anne, an orphaned twelve-year-old who was shuffled between lackluster families, but Anne finally lands in a permanent home with Marilla Cuthbert. In the movie version of *Anne of Green Gables*, Anne tells Marilla, "I'm in the depths of despair. Haven't you ever been in the depths of despair?" Marilla replies, "I have not. To be in despair is to turn your back on God."[3] To avoid despair when in a wilderness—seek God in prayer, the Holy One who saw Hagar and sees you.

Sometimes, we can't seem to find the words to even pray. During those times, turn to the Psalms for words that have been prayed by others through the centuries, or keep a book such as *Breath Prayers for Women* at hand, which promises that simple whispers to God can keep you in his presence.[4]

Second, open your Bible and seek direction. The Bible gives us truthful testimony about God and his interactions with all people. Look for characters that experienced dilemmas similar to yours. As you read and study, ask for understanding and that God will lead you to information that guides you into his will. Try starting at James 3:15–17 (NIV), to see if your planned solutions match: "But the wisdom that comes from heaven is first of all pure; then peace-loving, considerate, submissive, full of mercy and good fruit, impartial and sincere."

Third, seek godly counsel. "Plans fail for lack of counsel, but with many advisers they succeed" (Prov. 15:22 NIV). You may want to seek counsel from several godly people after you have done the work of prayer in your dark night of the soul. Some seekers are spiritually lazy and skip praying and reading God's Word. Instead, they go directly to friends who have a sturdy walk of faith. We caution you to do the work of *during* prayer and Bible reading first, so you will know if you receive godly counsel.

Even after receiving counsel, match the counsel against God's Word. Remember, Moses sent spies into Canaan, and ten men intimidated by the land's inhabitants came back and counseled Moses not to move forward, which was contrary to God's commands. However, Joshua and Caleb trusted the promises of God and advised conquering Canaan. If Moses had followed the lead of the majority, Israel wouldn't have entered the Promised Land. Always compare any counsel to God's Word and wisdom.

In a wilderness or alone in a dark night—pray, read Scripture, and seek counsel.

My Combat Mission This Week
Lift up your eyes and watch for God's leading.

Historical Field Guide

Grace Livingston Hill, 1867–1947, was born in New York to a Presbyterian minister and his wife one day after the death of Abraham Lincoln, and Grace's religious upbringing would heavily influence her one hundred novels and articles. She wrote her first novel at the age of twenty, and she later wrote to earn money for a family vacation. From that experience, she established a habit: when she was short on cash, she wrote a novel.

She found herself in a desert place after her husband Frank died of appendicitis, and she had the burden to support her two children and her mother. She wrote and sold stories to bring money into their poor household. She eventually adopted a style of writing that appealed to general readers but proclaimed a clear gospel message. She became the forerunner of now-popular inspirational fiction.

In her novel *The Girl from Montana* (1922), a girl fled her childhood home where the dad forbade any religious training, but her late mother had instilled only one Psalm in the girl's heart: "For in the time of trouble he shall hide me in his pavilion: in the secret of his tabernacle shall he hide me; he shall set me up upon a rock" (Ps. 27:5 KJV). The heroine embarked on a journey on horseback from the West all the way to Philadelphia. Throughout the perilous travel, that one verse kept reverberating in her heart as she literally saw it come true in her life. She recognized that she was protected and directed by the hand of God.

Perhaps that verse meant so much to Grace Livingston because of her own heartache and needing direction. Her grandson reported about a second marriage at the age of thirty-nine, where in a "rare show of bad judgment," Grace married a twenty-four-year-old high-strung man, Flavius, who was a "weak candidate for marriage." Later, dinnertime turned into "a cockpit with the rooster attacking the hens," where the females endured verbal abuse. Grace did not believe in divorce, but Flavius eventually left and never came back. Grace kept on writing, and perhaps her failed marriage was fodder for her novel *Blue Ruin*.

Her daughters married godly men, and all four of her grandchildren had careers in missions or church leadership. Her grandson, Munce, "believes that, given a chance to sum up her own remarkable career, she would say merely, 'Thank you, God, for using me.'"[5]

My Combat Prayer

Father, please direct and speak tenderly to me in my wilderness.

*I will allure her, and bring her into the wilderness,
and speak tenderly to her (Hosea 2:14).*

Tactical Training

1. Hagar had few personal freedoms because she was a servant in Abram and Sarai's household. Read Acts 17:24–28. What

134

do you discover about the time and place of our lives, about history and boundaries?

2. The accepted cultural practices where Hagar lived complicated her life and brought circumstances over which she had no control. Have you experienced a personal loss of freedom because of the place and time you live?

3. Some human suffering occurs because of others' sins. Read 2 Samuel 21:1–14. Why did Rizpah suffer? What other Bible mothers or characters suffered because of the sins of others?

4. Sins and wrong decisions can have far-reaching consequences and affect a family for generations. Read Jeremiah 35. This family had a good outcome for years, because their ancestor (Jehonadab son of Rekab) gave great family guidelines.

5. God appeared and gave Hagar hope and direction. Read Romans 15:13 and recall a time when God poured hope into your fears. By what means did he accomplish rebuilding your hope?

6. Hagar seems caught up in two dramas: Abram's family dynamics and her own dilemmas. Psalm 27:5 makes a bold declaration that in a time of trouble, God will hide you in

his secret pavilion, and set your feet upon a rock. When has God sheltered you during a storm and sent you in a specific direction?

7. God said to the prophet Jeremiah, "Call to me and I will answer you, and will tell you great and hidden things that you have not known" (Jer. 33:3). Do you ever become obsessed with what tomorrow holds? Do you believe God will let you know what you need to know?

8. Winning woman, always seek direction and clarity during a personal spiritual or physical crisis. Imagine God asking you the same question he asked Hagar: "Where have you come from? Where are you going?" Be honest in your answer and then seek his loving direction.

My Diary from the Trenches

Expect your heavenly Father's guiding light to shine on your path as you pray, study, and seek counsel. Record your victories.

Chapter Nine

Intercession with Gratitude

Paul

"Continue steadfastly in prayer." —Colossians 4:2

Hurting, lost, and desperate people come into contact with us every day. They stand in line behind us at the grocery store, haggard and desolate. They sit behind us in a church pew, tearful and worried. They lay in hospital beds—lonely, scared, without visitors or advocates. Compassionate women long to make a difference, lift a burden, or right a wrong. Women love to fix things for broken people, but that often results in burned-up energies and frustrations. Too often prayer becomes the last battle cry instead of the first line of attack.

Battles fought for the lost, hurting, and distraught begin and end at the throne of Almighty God. Swords slung through our own strength cause no damage to the invading enemy troops, but swords raised by the power of the Holy Spirit accessed by prayer can do amazingly more than we could imagine. Battles are won when women choose prayer before activity. Activity may show tangible results in our chosen timeline, but prayer changes lives and hearts, making an eternal, not just physical, difference. As we set our eyes on things above, placing value on the eternal, our battle strategy becomes clear: pray and wait on God's timing, will, and direction. He fights alongside us when we remember to ask.

Paul—the Praying Apostle

The prayers of Abraham and Moses in earlier chapters taught us the value of intercession by example. Paul also prayed for others, plus he gave instruction and pleas for intercession. His life, radically lived, shows evidence of his strong petitions.

Paul boldly introduced himself in Acts 22:3–4 (NIV) to a group of Jews who want to kill him: "I am a Jew, born in Tarsus of Cilicia, but brought up in this city. I studied under Gamaliel and was thoroughly trained in the law of our ancestors. I was just as zealous for God as any of you are today. I persecuted the followers of this Way to their death, arresting both men and women and throwing them into prison."

In Philippians 3, Paul told us a little more about himself: "Circumcised on the eighth day, of the people of Israel, of the tribe of Benjamin, a Hebrew of Hebrews; as to the law, a Pharisee; as to zeal, a persecutor of the church; as to righteousness under the law, blameless" (Phil. 3:5–6).

Paul, a type A personality, lived a life full of passion. If he did something, he did it with all he had. No halfway attempts for him. And finally, Paul gave us another glimpse into his exterior and interior perils in 2 Corinthians 11:23–28.

> Are they servants of Christ? I am a better one—I am
> talking like a madman—with far greater labors, far more

imprisonments, with countless beatings, and often near
death. Five times I received at the hands of the Jews the
forty lashes less one. Three times I was beaten with rods.
Once I was stoned. Three times I was shipwrecked; a
night and a day I was adrift at sea; on frequent journeys,
in danger from rivers, danger from robbers, danger
from my own people, danger from Gentiles, danger in
the city, danger in the wilderness, danger at sea, danger
from false brothers; in toil and hardship, through many
a sleepless night, in hunger and thirst, often without
food, in cold and exposure. And, apart from other
things, there is the daily pressure on me of my anxiety
for all the churches.

This bragging tirade, used by Paul as evidence of his apostleship,
revealed his incredible hardships. From biblical descriptions of
Paul, one thing becomes clear—the passionate Paul walked out
everything God asked of him. He jumped in cannonball-style,
regardless of possible circling sharks. So when Paul says "pray
without ceasing" (1 Thess. 5:17), that is what he meant and did.

Paul's call into ministry began with a convincing demon-
stration of intercessory prayer's power. Paul, named Saul at that
time, left Jerusalem "breathing threats and murder against the
disciples of the Lord" (Acts 9:1). He traveled toward Damascus
with the same vile intentions, but God met him on the journey,
and Paul's life underwent an extensive transformation. Blinded
on the road by God's power, shocked by the words of Jesus, Saul
had to be led by the hand as he stumbled into Damascus. Jesus
promised he would send someone to give Saul instructions,
so Saul sat three days in darkness with a stomach emptied by

fasting. Then Ananias arrived at God's direction and laid hands on Saul, who was filled with the Holy Spirit and had his vision restored. God renamed him Paul, and he went from being a persecutor of Christians to a Christian persecuted.

Paul preached and lived what he knew to be true—prayer to God changes situations, lives, and hearts. His prayers for the fledgling church were the most important thing he could give them. In his letters, he reveals his intercessory prayers, requests their prayers, and entreats them to pray continually. Intercessory prayer mattered to Paul. He saw the power it brought and the fruit it produced. Prayer does what women cannot do, even if we had limitless energy and resources.

Paul's Prayers

Paul's prayers for the churches varied depending on his audience, just as prayer warriors pray according to specific needs. Paul prayed and let churches know his petitions: for Corinth—"Your restoration is what we pray for" (2 Cor. 13:9); for Philippi—"It is my prayer that your love may abound more and more, with knowledge and all discernment, so that you may approve what is excellent, and so be pure and blameless for the day of Christ" (Phil. 1:9–10); for Thessalonica—"We always pray for you, that our God may make you worthy of his calling and may fulfill every resolve for good and every work of faith by his power" (2 Thess. 1:11); and for the church in Ephesus—"For this reason I bow my knees before the Father . . . that according to the riches of his glory he may grant you to be strengthened with power through his Spirit in your inner being, so that Christ may dwell in your hearts through faith—that you, being rooted and grounded in love, may have strength to comprehend with all the saints what is the breadth and length and height and depth, and to know the love of Christ" (Eph. 3:14–19).

Paul desired to spread God's truth through discipleship. He assisted inexperienced churches and instructed them as they grew, and a vital thread in this discipleship tapestry was prayer. This pattern repeated often: Paul prayed for them, taught them to pray, and requested their prayers. Prayer was the vibrant thread that held the young church together. Prayer brought the power of God into weak and fragile communities of believers, creating a masterpiece that eventually changed the world.

In the Trenches with Deanna: My mom fought breast cancer two different times, finally losing the battle with cancer, yet gaining her crown of eternal life. During those battles, my mom received hundreds of cards, some funny, some serious, but all encouraging. Some cards showcased cartoon characters while others displayed magnificent scenery. Regardless of the theme of the card, the senders always let her know she was in their prayers and dearly loved. The cards usually contained Scripture promises or specific prayers: "I'm praying for complete healing," "Praying God gives you grace and strength," "I pray you feel God's love and comfort," "May God do more than you could ask or imagine." Six years after my mom's death, my dad still has three full baskets containing these cards in his living room, a tangible reminder of faithful friends and the power of prayer.

During Mom's battle, I sent out frequent updates through emails letting friends and family know the latest information on her journey. After an update, my inbox would fill with words of encouragement from those who loved us. I saved every reply, and I often read them when feeling overwhelmed. God used those emails, cards, and prayers as sustenance for my mom then and me now. Those intercessors prayed for us, encouraged us, and helped us carry the heavy burden of a cancer battle.

Prayer remains one of the greatest gifts we can give, and we add an additional kindness when we let the receiver know of our prayers. That time taught me so much about grace, God's timing, will, and the importance of maintaining an eternal perspective. The value of intercession and encouragement was reinforced, and those cards and emails represent not only prayers but love—the precious love we share with one another.

My Dog Tag

"_____, keep alert with all perseverance, making supplication for all the saints" (Eph. 6:18).

In the Trenches with Jesus: Jesus washed his disciples' feet, shared the Passover dinner, left Jerusalem, and walked east to the Mount of Olives. John 17 records some of the words and prayers of Jesus as they made this short journey together, the last words to them before his arrest, crucifixion, and resurrection.

Jesus told them to love one another, promised the Holy Spirit, explained the importance of remaining in him, and prayed for them. His prayer was not just for those twelve but also for us who believe as a result of their testimony (John 17:20).

Jesus's prayer, often called the High Priestly Prayer, entreats God for believers everywhere. When Jesus intercedes for us in this prayer, he asks that we be one, just as he is one with the Father. His desire for unity is stated multiple times, for our unity witnesses to the world that God sent Jesus. Unity draws attention to God (21). Jesus also asks God to keep us from the evil one (15).

He requests that we be set apart in truth (17), and finally, he ends his prayer asking God to fill us with his love and with his Spirit (26). The power and love that only Jesus can provide helps us walk in unity, avoid evil, and live set-apart lives. Along with his continual intercession, he equips us to fully live in the world as the body of Christ.

When we love others as Christ loved us, our immediate response will be intercessory prayer.

Armor of God

Sword: "_____, continue steadfastly in prayer, being watchful in it with thanksgiving" (Col. 4:2).

Shield: "_____, encourage one another and build one another up, just as you are doing (1 Thess. 5:11).

Shoes: "_____, above all these put on love, which binds everything together in perfect harmony" (Col. 3:14).

When We Don't Know What to Pray

Prayer requests differ just as much as those who request. One may ask for healing, another begs for provision, while someone else seeks peace. One person might crave prayer but never ask, while another doesn't realize she desperately needs prayer. Sometimes the direction a prayer should take seems obvious, but when a different need arises, it is hard to know where to start and what to ask.

At all times our prayers should be led by the Spirit just as we walk by the Spirit (Eph. 6:18). God, through his Spirit living inside of us, directs our prayers according to his will and his ways. A woman who longs to engage in Spirit-directed prayer will learn to wait. Waiting is the key. Not waiting to pray but waiting while in prayer. Pray as the Spirit places people or events on your heart or in your mind. Let him guide your time in his presence. Believe and embrace this truth: "The Spirit helps us in our weakness. For we do not know what to pray for as we ought, but the Spirit himself intercedes for us with groanings too deep for words" (Rom. 8:26). When we turn our hearts toward God, his Spirit goes before us and cleans up our jumbled and fumbled petitions and presents them sparkly pure at the throne of grace.

In the Trenches with Cathy: Deanna and I had a one-week book launch when our first co-authored book debuted, *Winning Every Woman's War: Defeating Temptations.* We created an event on Facebook with prizes and books to give away, and then we sent out invitations. The prizes included *Inspire* Bibles, a camo pink tote and T-shirt, coffee mug and coffee, and another ten or so faith-based gifts. To determine winners, we asked participants to post replies to our questions. They posted pictures of themselves in camo, they told why their personal Bibles were favorites, and they named a camo-dressed mannequin we use in presentations. We also asked them to take a photo and post it of their favorite shoes because of the Armor of God sword, shield, and shoe sections in our book. We had good participation and enjoyed gifting the prizes and copies of our book.

One day during the contest, we asked our Facebook audience if they had prayer requests we could honor. Their response was greater than any that week. They wanted to defeat fears, find straight paths, and ask for God's will to replace their will. They asked for physical healing, to know God more fully, for homeschooling to go well. One wanted a stalker to go away, another to relieve family problems, and more. When one woman asks another, "How may I pray for you?" a spiritual connection takes place like no other. When I offer to pray or ask a woman to pray for me, I am more connected to those women than others.

Recently, I phoned a young woman and asked, "How may I pray for you today?" She responded right away, "That God remove any pride, make me humble, and make me kind." She had noticed her ragged edges and wanted her loving Father to reshape her into the image of Jesus. Women who pray intercessory prayers for others partner with our brother Paul, who prayed for the church at Philippi: "I always pray with joy because of your partnership in the gospel . . . being confident of this, that he who began a good work in you will carry it on to completion until the day of Christ Jesus" (Phil. 1:4–6 NIV).

Praying soldiers, please intercede for others always . . . because that's when you reach God, who makes the difference in our small worlds, this world, and the next.

Responding and Releasing

Faithful prayer warriors often find themselves bombarded with entreaties from many because we live in a broken and fallen world forever in need of prayer. We could easily get pulled into a hole of utter despair by the weighty darkness swirling around us, but being buried under this pressure would render us less than the best intercessors.

When a private prayer request arrives, it must then move on. The request does not move to the gossip column at the neighborhood church or onto a Facebook post. The path moves from the one who requests, to us, and then on to God. We do not keep it nor let the request become our burden. We leave needs at the foot of God's throne of mercy and walk away empty-handed, yet with a heart full of peace. We may have cause to deliver the same request numerous times until we learn to leave the need with God.

How do you know to make a return trip to the throne room? If you find yourself stressing about the situation, you will know that you have grabbed the problem back into your unqualified hands. Requests belong to God. He alone can answer correctly. No good purpose comes from a request clasped in fretting, fisted fingers. Our fingers are pried loose as we pray, moving requests from feeble hands to God's abundant store of provision.

What a blessing to intercede in faith for others and place their needs in God's capable hands. Prayer warriors serve as messengers moving through enemy lines for the sake of our wilting and weary fellow soldiers.

Combat Mission for This Week
Pray daily for a sister in Christ this week and then send her an encouraging note.

Historical Field Guide

He preached to thousands every Sunday in England for over forty years. His quotes, sermons, and prayers are still published and read today by countless Christians. Charles Spurgeon, born in 1834, wrote numerous books and commentaries. He was called both the Prince of Preachers and the People's Preacher, and he could obviously deliver a powerful message from God through which thousands heard the gospel.

D. L. Moody traveled four thousand miles to hear Spurgeon preach in the fall of 1892. "What impressed him most was not the praise, though he thought he had never heard such grand congregational singing; it was not Mr. Spurgeon's exposition, fine though it was, nor even his sermon; it was his prayer."[1] He commented further, "He seemed to have such access to God that he could bring down the power from heaven; that was the great secret of his influence and success."

Charles Spurgeon could speak dynamically because he spent an abundance of time speaking to his Heavenly Father. Following is a portion of Spurgeon's prayer during a church service on November 4, 1877:

> Oh to love the Savior with a passion that can never
> cool. Oh to believe in God with a confidence that can
> never stagger! Oh to hope in God with an expectation
> that can never dim! Oh to delight in God with holy
> overflowing rejoicing that can never be stopped, so that
> we might live to glorify God at the highest bent of our
> powers, living with enthusiasm, burning, blazing, being
> consumed with the indwelling of God who worketh all
> things according to his will!

Read more of Spurgeon's prayers in *The Pastor in Prayer*. Spurgeon often prayed for the works of the church, the Sunday school classes, the Christian college, the children in orphanages, the missionaries, the church both near and far, and the lost, and finally he would conclude by asking for God's kingdom to come. Like Paul, Charles Spurgeon understood prayer and the great need to pray for all people.

My Combat Prayer

Father, give me a constant heart that prays diligently for others.

Pray for one another (James 5:16).

Tactical Training

1. When you think of the Apostle Paul, what comes to mind? Take time this week to read one of his letters. Several are very short, yet packed with practical truths for daily living.

2. You may or may not be an "extreme" person like Paul, but you can still have an extreme prayer life. Being spiritually lazy can cripple your walk with God and obstruct your prayer life. What are some steps you can take this week to energize your prayer time—moving it to a place of vibrancy and vitality?

3. Do people often ask for your prayers? Are you faithful to pray? Commit to praying immediately upon getting a request and then again as God lays them on your heart. Let them know you have prayed; a snail-mail note of encouragement surely makes the mailbox a brighter place.

4. Consider again the High Priestly Prayer in John 17. The components are crucial for the church. What parts could you add to your daily prayer as you pray for Christians worldwide? Choose one prayer goal from John 17, and pray the same desires that are close to the heart of God.

5. Consider the following guidance prompts from Paul. Who could you pray these requests over today? Pray as the Spirit guides and directs your prayers: *Pray for salvation* (Rom. 10:1). *Ask that God will crush Satan under their feet* (Rom. 16:20). *Ask that God will sustain them* (1 Cor. 1:8). *Ask that they faithfully endure temptation and successfully resist* (1 Cor. 10:13). *Pray for daily renewal in Christ* (2 Cor. 4:16).

6. Paul was an apostle (apostle means one sent out), and as he corresponded with the churches, he regularly asked for prayers. The prayers of the church strengthened him and prepared hearts for the message of Christ. Partner with others who are sent and pray for them. Get a list of missionaries that your church supports. Be intentional in your prayers for them.

7. Do you ever awaken during the night, unable to sleep? Make a practice of using this time to pray for people as God brings them to mind. This is a great way to allow the Holy Spirit to

guide your prayers. If you are a sound sleeper (we are jealous), you can practice this at other times such as driving or doing chores. Ask God to bring persons to mind for whom you can intercede, and then allow him to direct the request.

8. Anna of Luke 2:36–40 was a great woman of prayer. Read her story. When you think of great women of prayer, who comes to mind? Do you have friends in your life who consistently lift you up to God? Pray for them, and then let them know how thankful you are for them and their prayers.

My Diary from the Trenches

Expect to pray Spirit-led prayers this week. Record your victories.

Chapter Ten

Seeking Forgiveness After Sins Committed

David

> "Blessed is the man against whom the LORD counts no iniquity,
> and in whose spirit there is no deceit." —Psalm 32:2

If you ask boys and girls to name another person in David's life, they will shout "Goliath!" If you ask an adult Bible class to name a person in David's life, many will say "Bathsheba."

The young David had a strong prayer life when he encountered Goliath, and he looked to the unseen hand of God for rescue. Instead of trembling in the presence of the oversized bully, David arrived to battle the giant enemy in the name of the Lord.

The aged David became careless, took Uriah's wife, shed innocent blood, and then tried to hide and undo the consequences of his sin. Eugene Peterson says, "In the encounter with Bathsheba, David recovers his identity as a person of prayer." David is no longer an innocent youth with fresh faith. He's a warrior, a king, a conqueror, who has a "multilayered" life that has "tangled and intermingled complexities of guilt and grace."[1]

151

Several books of the Bible tell the exterior stories of David's life, while the psalms he wrote tell his interior story. Specifically, David's exterior story about his adultery, further sin, repentance, and consequences are found in 2 Samuel 11 and 12, while the lyrics of Psalm 51 detail what was going on his heart.

David didn't suddenly commit adultery. He had many opportunities to turn his back on the temptation of lust. Most kings went to war in the springtime, but David remained in Jerusalem at his palace. While walking on his rooftop, he looked upon a woman bathing. He could have honorably turned away, but Satan would have his way that evening. David watched her as she bathed, likely performing her ritual of purification after her monthly cycle.

He asked a servant about the woman. The man said, "Isn't this Bathsheba, the daughter of Eliam, the wife of Uriah the Hittite?" (2 Sam. 11:3). The man spoke a plain warning to David, by mentioning the names of some of David's closest companions, who were also related to Bathsheba: her father (Eliam), and her husband (Uriah). First, Eliam was the son of Ahithophel, one of David's current trusted advisors. Eliam was also listed as one of David's mighty warriors, and Bathsheba's husband Uriah was counted among those military elite soldiers who proved their allegiance to David (2 Sam. 23). These comrades were "David's mighty men, who gave him strong support in his kingdom, together with all Israel, to make him king" (1 Chron. 11:10; 11–47).

David sinned against God and valiant friends, who had risked their lives when he was on the run from King Saul. David dug a deep gutter that would require forgiveness from God and his faithful friends. When the consequences of his sin were evident, David plotted a cover-up by calling Uriah home from battle, thinking the man would visit his wife, Bathsheba, and sleep with her, but the honorable Uriah wouldn't because the soldiers he served with were without their wives and still in danger. Determined to deny his own pleasure, he said, "Shall I then go to my house, to eat and to drink and to lie with my wife? As you live, and as your soul lives, I will not do this thing" (2 Sam. 11:6–13).

The next night David plied Uriah with food and wine and made him drunk, but Uriah still wouldn't go to his house and bed his wife. David could have confessed to Uriah, but instead he chose the dim path of deceit. He had Uriah carry a sealed letter, his own death warrant, to his commander Joab. Joab, at King David's command, moved Uriah to the hottest part of the battle, so he would die at the hands of enemies.

After Bathsheba had mourned her husband, usually a seven-day period (Gen. 50:10; 1 Sam. 31:13), David brought her into the palace as his wife. After a baby son was born, God confronted David through Nathan the prophet. He told a story about a poor man who had one lamb and a rich man who had cattle and herds. He said the rich man took the one lamb and feasted upon it. God's engaging story shows his concern for Bathsheba and was perfectly suited to the former shepherd David, who had protected single lambs from disasters. When King David heard the story, he was furious at the injustice and said the man would die and repay four times the worth of the lamb. Nathan pointedly said, "You are the man!" (2 Sam. 12:7).

Armor of God

Sword: "Have mercy on _____, O God, according to your steadfast love; according to your abundant mercy blot out my transgressions (Ps. 51:1).

Shield: "Purge _____ with hyssop, and I shall be clean; wash _____, and I shall be whiter than snow" (Ps. 51:7).

Shoes: "Restore to _____ the joy of your salvation, and uphold _____ with a willing spirit" (Ps. 51:12).

Psalm 51—David's *After* Prayer Seeks Forgiveness

Oswald Chambers said, "We are only what we are in the dark; all the rest is reputation. What God looks at is what we are in the dark—the imaginations of our minds; the thoughts of our heart; the habits of our bodies; these are the things that mark us in God's sight."[2]

The attribution at Psalm 51 says David wrote that song of deliverance after Nathan had confronted him about his sins. David lamented his sins against God, mentioned his suffering and remorse, detailed his interior cleansing, and used the metaphor of washing with hyssop (known for antiseptic qualities) that would make him "whiter than snow." With inward repentance, David sought forgiveness and again experienced reconnection to the holiness of God. His ancient words—refreshed by a new melody—are sung by congregations worldwide. The relevant words, "Create in me a clean heart, O God," have touched hearts for centuries, stirring repentance, causing us to seek the washing that only the pierced hands of God provide. God always notices when a woman comes to him and offers a "broken and contrite heart."

Praise his holy name. That sacrifice, "O God, you will not despise."

In the Trenches with Deanna: "I am so, so sorry, please forgive me!" These words were the most common utterances from my mouth during a rough season in my twenties. However, the problem wasn't continual sin, it was the repetition of asking forgiveness for one especially serious sin. I couldn't seem to accept forgiveness. I knew God could and would forgive if asked, but due to the nature of this sin and the guilt it produced, I just would not accept forgiveness. The sin, that I was no longer engaged in, still ruled over me. I remained captive, as it tore at me daily, bringing depression and self-loathing. I was a mess.

Breaking Free, a Bible study by Beth Moore, gave me the weapons of warfare that I needed. During this study, I realized many valuable truths that still serve me today. Guilt is a tool of the enemy, not something God doles out to his children. I also realized the pride involved in not accepting forgiveness. And finally, I discovered it was not for me to forgive myself but simply for me to accept the forgiveness from God that came at an incredible price—the brutal death of his only Son.

Guilt often led me to question my forgiveness and my value. Nothing I could ever do would change God's love for me. While the Holy Spirit does convict us of sin, he does not want us to fall captive to guilt. God wanted the sin stopped and for me to walk in obedience, but he never desired guilt or shame to enslave me. The enemy tried to move me from one prison to another barred cell. Now when those feelings surface, I recognize them and take them captive by choosing to believe I am forgiven and my sins were removed, as far from me as the east is from the west.

The pride piece of the puzzle shocked me. I really believed it was humility that drove me to see myself as not worth forgiving. After what I knew myself to be capable of, how could I walk in pride? Unfortunately, I found a way. Pride made me believe my sin was the one unforgivable sin; somehow my transgression was beyond the blood of Christ. Once this lie was exposed, God quickly defeated it with truth. I was appalled that I had bought into this scheme of the enemy, but thankfully I did not wallow in guilt. I asked for and accepted forgiveness. I was learning, even if a little slowly.

One frequent line spoken to myself during this time was "I just can't forgive myself." And apparently I thought God couldn't forgive me until I did. Looking back I see lots of holes in this logic. Nowhere in Scripture does God instruct us to forgive ourselves so that he can then forgive us. Forgiveness does not hinge on me—it's all about the blood shed at the cross. And if God who is holy and perfect chooses to forgive me, who am I to deny myself forgiveness?

My Dog Tag

"Declare _____ innocent from hidden faults. Keep back your servant also from presumptuous sins; let them not have dominion over me! Then _____ shall be blameless, and innocent of great transgression" (Ps. 19:12–13).

I am extremely thankful for the timeliness of Beth Moore's study that taught me and revealed the crafty schemes of the enemy.

I still stub my toe on a few of his traps, but typically I quickly recall my forgiveness and recognize the value of Christ's sacrifice, and then I no longer allow the enemy to let me consider myself beyond forgiveness.

In the Trenches with Jesus: Our Savior never had to ask forgiveness because he didn't sin. However, he daily bumped elbows with women and men who needed forgiveness for every conceivable wrong. For the rest of our lives, we will need pardon from God because we will sin against him and others, and Jesus plainly said, "Forgive us our debts as we forgive our debtors, or as *The Message* says, "Keep us forgiven with you and forgiving others" (Matt. 6:12). Latayne C. Scott says this is not "theological tit-for-tat." God's work of forgiveness is ongoing as is our work of forgiveness. Scott continues, "That makes a grudge the most expensive thing our souls can buy."[3]

Jesus taught a principle of communal forgiveness: "And when you stand praying, if you hold anything against anyone, forgive them, so that your Father in heaven may forgive you your sins" (Mark 11:25 NIV). The disciples must have struggled with forgiveness as much as we do. Matthew Henry says, "Though we live wholly on mercy and forgiveness, we are backward to forgive the offences of our brethren." Among rabbis during Jesus's time, the consensus was that a person must forgive three times. This teaching was perhaps based on Amos 1:3–13, where God mentions that after three offenses, even four, that he would not hold back his wrath from offending cities and nations. Bible scholars agree that the "three" and "four" mentioned in Amos's warning are not arithmetic numbers, but represent "frequent transgressions" or "multiplied or repeated delinquencies."[4]

In generous allowance, Peter asked: "Lord, how many times shall I forgive my brother when he sins against me? Up to seven times?" Jesus's answer went beyond the law, beyond current thought, and beyond the grace of even "seventy-seven" (Matt. 18:15–22). The Jewish disciples would have recognized the numbers "seven" and "seventy-seven" from the Old Testament stories of Cain and Lamech, who both shed blood in revenge. Lamech boasted, "I have killed a man for wounding me, a young man for striking me. If Cain's revenge is sevenfold, then Lamech's is seventy-sevenfold" (Gen. 4:1–18; 23–24). They killed in over-the-top revenge. Peter heard the Lord call him to lavish forgiveness. Revenge is the easy road, the well-worn path the world has beaten out. Unrestrained forgiveness is the less traveled path that leads straight to the heart of God.

More than three, more than seven, more than seventy-seven—God offers unlimited forgiveness. No one can out-forgive God! The disciples walked with the wonderful, merciful Savior, yet they still thought in arithmetic numbers, keeping a score of wrongs, but perfect love keeps no record of wrongs. The question for women who receive God's generous and daily forgiveness is: Do we forgive a repeat offender the tenth time with as much grace as we did the first time? Jesus calls us to that high standard.

> When God gets us alone through suffering,
> heartbreak, temptation, disappointment, sickness,
> or by thwarted friendship—when He gets us
> absolutely alone, and we are totally speechless,
> unable to ask even one question, then He begins
> to teach us. —Oswald Chambers

> Never does the human soul appear so strong as when it forgoes revenge, and dares forgive an injury.[5] —E. H. Chapin

Bathsheba

Her Hebrew name *Bat-Sheva* meant "daughter of the oath." We wonder about Bathsheba and if she harbored resentment: she was called by King David to his bed, she became pregnant by the king, then David had her husband killed and took her as his wife, and the child conceived by adultery died. Jewish tradition says she later composed Proverbs 31, about a virtuous woman, for her second son Solomon when he married the Pharaoh's daughter.[6]

On the night of her encounter with King David, Bathsheba was most likely performing her purification ceremony after her monthly cycle, which would have placed her at the most fertile time of the month (Lev. 15:19–29). Today, an Orthodox Jewish menstruating woman abstains from touching her husband during her period, even when handing him a glass of water. When her flow has ceased, she participates in the cleansing immersion ritual. She fully bathes before traveling to her community's Mikveh, a collection or gathering of waters. She recites Scripture as she leaves her home and travels to Mikveh.

Upon arrival at Mikveh, she totally immerses herself in the cleansing waters, and during her return home, she again recites Scripture before reuniting with her husband. As many do, she might remind herself that God is central to her life, and God separated her people from the womb of the world. Indeed, God says in Isaiah that he carried Israel in his womb, birthed them, and continually cared for them (Isa. 49:14–15)—powerful imagery, birthed into the world but not of the world.

Every day, national news reminds us about the ugliness of revenge in our world. For inspiration to forgive others, turn to God's Word for accurate truth about the weight of sin, the fellowship of repentance, *after* prayers for reconciliation, and the joy of God's forgiveness and openhandedness to us even when we have wronged him. Allow him to give you a new birth in Christ—a new creation that forgives as God forgives.

God's Generosity

When Nathan the prophet confronted David about his sin, God sent a personal message about a desire to bless David: "I anointed you king over Israel, and I delivered you from the hand of Saul. I gave your master's house to you, and your master's wives into your arms. I gave you all Israel and Judah. And if all this had been too little, I would have given you even more. Why did you despise the word of the LORD by doing what is evil in his eyes?" (2 Sam. 12:7–9 NIV).

While David would suffer future consequences of his sin, overwhelming love and bigheartedness showed up during God's rebuke: "And if all this had been too little, I would have given you even more." Do you struggle to understand God's out-of-this world love that gives . . . gives again . . . and wants to give us more? Even when we've treated him with shabby contempt? After Nathan's rebuke, David said, "I have sinned against the Lord" (13).

Nathan answered immediately, "The LORD also has put away your sin." God's forgiveness and other resources allow us to move on from a grievous sin and still accomplish God's will in our lives. God loves you and David equally; do you hear him saying this to you? "If all I've given you is too little, I will give you more." When we imagine God's gentle voice saying that to us, tears spring to our eyes.

Learn that. Believe that. His mercy, grace, resources, and forgiveness are available to all and withheld from none who seek his face.

In the Trenches with Cathy: One of the most humbling things for a follower of Christ is to find out that your heart isn't as pure as you thought. That happened to me a few years back when I kept silent and let an interviewer think an event happened on a certain day when it had actually happened the day before. It wasn't in a court of law, but it did involve a law of the land. The deception wouldn't cause anyone dire harm, but as the interview went on a few minutes, I knew I couldn't let him misunderstand the time frame. I told him the truth of when the event happened. I apologized for allowing my silence to mislead him.

As far as I know, no harm came from that lapse in truth, but I felt extreme shame that I had given into that temptation. I had an immediate conviction from the Holy Spirit that my silence was wrong. I also had a rude awakening about how quickly I could step off the path of right living and consider deception an option. I prayed for pardon as I drove home and lamented over my sin. I knew intellectually that immediate forgiveness was mine, yet my regret from the lapse of good judgment left me fretting. Even after repentance and receiving God's forgiveness, I remained disappointed in my behavior and the knowledge that what I'd done sprang from "unfinished" places in my heart.

When I returned home, I phoned a woman who is my close friend, and I confessed to her. My confession and her patient listening is what I needed to heal and move forward. She's the kind of friend who wouldn't desert me because of this confession. My friend's response was stellar. She remained calm. She allowed me to accuse myself and name my sin. She didn't say, "Oh, that's okay. We all do that at times." She didn't offer excuses for my behavior. She didn't say the sin was trite, "Oh, that's nothing." She allowed my guilt and remorse to do the work God intended. And she did the work God planned for her—

—She forgave me. She loved me. She received my hurt. She helped restore my soul.

Choosing Forgiveness

Each time we are wronged, we have choices to make. We can seek revenge, we can harbor a grudge, we can become bitter, or we can choose to forgive. Revenge, grudges, and bitterness negatively affect our minds and our bodies, and an unforgiving spirit damages, sometimes irrevocably, our witness that we are members of God's family and Jesus is our Savior.

Not forgiving is like a barking dog. You hate its continual yapping, but it's a pet and you don't want to get rid of it, either. The pride of "I'm right. You're wrong" keeps you bedding down with a woofing dog and fleas. Revenge bites and itches, and the scratching cycle keeps us irritated. We suggest the following seven steps to forgiveness.

1. Recognize your unforgiving spirit. Do you feel resentful toward someone? Are you angry, bitter, or insulted? How long have you been annoyed by an offense? (Eph. 4:31).
2. Recall God's mercy and how much he has forgiven you (Ps. 32:5).

3. Confess and repent of not forgiving, and then make the godly choice to forgive as you are forgiven (Matt. 6:12).
4. Place your hope of success in the fact that you have assistance to forgive. "I can do all things through him who strengthens me" (Phil. 4:13).
5. Bless the one who offended you through prayer and good deeds (Luke 6:27–29).
6. When the offending incident comes to mind again, and it will, examine to see if it is only a memory or if you still harbor bitterness. Immediately pray for release from any further resentment (1 John 1:9).
7. Rest in the peace that forgiving others brings (Prov. 16:7).

Nelson Mandela said, "Resentment is like drinking poison and then hoping it will kill your enemies." The Preacher said, "Although a wicked person who commits a hundred crimes may live a long time, I know that it will go better with those who fear God, who are reverent before him" (Eccl. 8:12 NIV).

Combat Mission for This Week
Ask for cleansing and then offer mercies as you have received mercies.

Historical Field Guide

In *Dark Journey Deep Grace: Jeffrey Dahmer's Story of Faith*, minister Roy Ratcliff tells about his visits with Jeffrey in prison, baptizing him, and their further Bible studies on forgiveness. Jeffrey Dahmer was tried and convicted of the grotesque murders of seventeen young men. The families of the deceased were horrified, bitter, and disgusted as details of their deaths emerged.

Some felt they could never forgive him. He was punished with fifteen consecutive life sentences because the state of Wisconsin didn't have the death penalty even for a monster who would rape, torture, mutilate, and cannibalize his victims.

After Dahmer's incarceration, two people sent him Bible correspondence courses, Curtis Booth and Mary Mott. After completing them, Dahmer requested baptism. Because Minister Roy Ratcliff lived near the prison, the chaplain at the maximum security prison contacted him to set a date to meet Dahmer. On April 20, 1994, Ratcliff was excited, but he was a bit apprehensive to meet this notorious person. They were able to sit in a small private room at a table, and after get-acquainted small talk, Ratcliff said, "I need to ask you an important question. Why do you want to be baptized?"

Dahmer had gone beyond the Bible correspondence studies and had read in the Bible the books of Mark, Romans, and Acts. He said that he believed in Jesus and wanted to be "buried with him in baptism," like Paul of Damascus, and have "his sins washed away." Convicted of Dahmer's repentance, confession, and belief, Ratcliff said he would baptize him. Then Dahmer breathed a huge sigh, and Ratcliff asked, "Why did you make that noise just now?"

Dahmer said, "I was nervous about meeting you today." Then he added, "I was afraid you would come and tell me that I couldn't be baptized because my sins are too evil." Roy assured him he would never do that. Permission and arrangements for the baptism would take time, and the chaplain thought they could use the prison whirlpool tub in the medical wing.

Ratcliff recalled two events of May 10, the day set for Dahmer's baptism: a noon solar eclipse threw the prison into a darkened state as he arrived. Also, the serial killer John Wayne Gacy, convicted of killing thirty-three people, was to be executed in Illinois on that same day. The irony of Dahmer's new birth and forgiveness was a stark contrast to other events of that day.

Ratcliff noticed the goodwill of guards and inmates, one even humming a hymn as they walked to the medical unit. Ratcliff requested to come once a week to study with Dahmer and help him further his faith. His request surprised Dahmer, who thought the minister would baptize him and then never return. They continued their studies until Dahmer's untimely death on Nov. 28, 1994, when another inmate killed him.

Roy spoke at Dahmer's memorial service about his baptism, their studies, and their friendship. He told of Dahmer's remorse and wishes that he could do something for his victims' families. Ratcliff said, "Many people were shocked and scandalized by his baptism, but I think their shock is really anger." Roy said it seemed those who were shocked that Jeff came to Christ would rather have Christ reject Dahmer and turn his back on him, but they didn't understand why Jesus came to earth—"to save sinners and Jeff was a sinner."

Ratcliff told the audience a story about a quiet girl asking, "Is heaven for little girls like me?" Then he said that's how he viewed Dahmer—standing on the outside, knowing his awful sins, and asking, "Is heaven for boys like me?"

Two sisters of a victim were present at the memorial. One had forgiven Dahmer; the other harbored bitterness and unforgiveness. Ratcliff closed with these remarks:

> Although we are involved in a memorial for Jeff, I want
> you to know that we care about your feelings, too. The

thing we are remembering here is that Jeff turned to God for forgiveness, and God is willing to forgive someone as bad as Jeff. I believe if Jeff were here right now, he would look at you and apologize for what he did to your brother. He was a changed man. He was being remade into the image of Jesus Christ.[7]

My Combat Prayer

Wash my heart and put a new song in my mouth.

He put a new song in my mouth, a song of praise to our God. Many will see and fear, and put their trust in the LORD (Ps. 40:3).

Tactical Training

1. Read Psalm 51. David's song shows his remorse, clearer thinking, and joy after forgiveness. What lines within that psalm have prompted other hymns we now sing? In verse 14, why did David ask God to save him from bloodguilt?

2. Read 2 Samuel 11 and 12, the story of David, Bathsheba, Uriah, and Nathan. Who suffered because of David's sin? How far-reaching were the effects of his sin? Under the old law, what should have happened to David? What results did God's forgiveness produce?

3.   Consider Peter's and Judas's sins of denial and betrayal of
     Jesus. Peter's heart broke when he realized his sin. Judas
     planned his sin for profit (thirty pieces of silver) and tol-
     erated his sin longer. How were their outcomes different?
     Why? (Peter—Matt. 26:69–75; Judas—John 13:21, 26–27,
     and Matt. 27:1–5)

4.   Read Matthew 6:12–15 and 18:32–34. Forgiveness is condi-
     tional to our forgiveness of others' offences. Do you harbor
     an unforgiving spirit? Will you repent?

5.   Read Colossians 3:12–14. What virtues are listed along with
     requisite forgiveness of each other?

6.   Do you find people more difficult to forgive if they are repeat
     offenders? Read Matthew 18:21–22. Do repeat offenders
     "deserve" forgiveness?

7.   Consider Jesus's forgiveness from the cross. Though in
     torture, pain, and absolute misery inflicted by enemies, he
     forgave them. Where would that kind of magnificent for-
     giveness work best in your life? Do you have enemies?

8. David's sin, repentance, and forgiveness are a familiar Bible story, but what in this story refreshed your understanding and prompted your desire to forgive as you are forgiven?

My Diary from the Trenches

Expect God to forgive your sins immediately as you confess. Forgive others as quickly. Record your victories.

Chapter Eleven

Thanksgiving After Deliverance

Daniel

"Give thanks in all circumstances; for this is the will of God in Christ Jesus for you." —1 Thessalonians 5:18

Emily Post, an etiquette authority, wrote fifty pages about thankfulness in one of her books. She advised readers when to send notes, how to write a note of thanks, and what to do when an expected thank-you note isn't received. A verbal or written thank you lets the giver know the gift or kindness was appreciated, not expected. Basic manners include verbal and written "thank yous," and the lack of those courtesies is considered rude. Children are taught to say "thank you" as some of their first words. Thankfulness is considered an attractive virtue, an intricate piece of propriety.

The two small words have great value. Are they really worth all that much? Possibly the words are not, but the attitude and disposition of gratitude are undeniable. When applied to prayer life, the value increases by massive proportions. When a prayerful woman regularly gives thanks to her Creator, she acknowledges where her blessings originate and who supplies her every need. A lack of thanksgiving often indicates self-reliance or an unfortunate sense of entitlement. When thanksgiving fails to ascend, worry and dissatisfaction often find a fertile place to grow. The *after* prayer of thanksgiving conditions the heart to be humble, satisfied, and generous.

Daniel's Deadly Dedication

Daniel, of noble blood and sterling character, has a book in the Old Testament named for him that divulges his remarkable story. Daniel came on the scene as a captive, a prisoner of war. Judah, his country, was conquered by the Babylonians, and the Jews, God's chosen people, were led away as spoils of war. Daniel, thanks to his royal lineage and attractive appearance, became part of the palace elite. The Babylonians educated and trained their young protégés for three years. Daniel was taught languages, culture, and literature, but he resolved from the start of captivity not to conform in any way that would defile him. He remained faithful to God.

Daniel's first deadly challenge came as the result of troubled sleep and a disturbing dream—not his dream, but King Nebuchadnezzar's. Upon awakening, the king of Babylon assembled his group of advisors and demanded not only an interpretation; he also wanted them to tell him the *content* of his dream. When those summoned confessed their inability, the enraged king swore to have every one of them "torn limb from limb" and their homes destroyed (Dan. 2:5). They attempted to explain the impossibility, but the king would not relent. The dream dilemma—a nightmarish situation for the royal advisors—was brought to Daniel's attention.

Daniel and his friends prayed and sought God's mercy and intervention. During the night, God revealed the dream *and* interpretation to Daniel. Daniel didn't rush off immediately, anxious to save his life; he stopped and gave thanks. He thanked God for wisdom and might and for the answers he needed.

Years later, Daniel faced a new trial that could again result in being torn apart. Daniel found favor with King Darius, the new king of the empire, and he was among one hundred twenty rulers in the kingdom. The king planned to set Daniel above all other rulers because he had an excellent spirit (Dan. 6:3). This was not a popular idea among his peers. The resentful, overlooked rulers plotted Daniel's downfall, but they could find nothing negative about him. The only characteristic about Daniel that stood out was his devotion to God. So his cunning enemies attacked his prayer life.

Without Daniel's knowledge, the schemers approached the king with a devious conspiracy. "All agreed that the king should issue an edict and enforce the decree that anyone who prays to any god or human being during the next thirty days, except to you, Your Majesty, shall be thrown into the lions' den" (Dan. 6:7 NIV). These conspirators surely cackled evil as they exited the throne room: their plan fed the king's ego, made them look loyal, and would be the downfall of their rival, Daniel.

"Now when Daniel learned that the decree had been published, he went home to his upstairs room where the windows opened toward Jerusalem. Three times a day he got down on his knees and prayed, giving thanks to his God, just as he had done before" (Dan. 6:10 NIV). He didn't fear physical danger. He didn't alter his time with God. Just as planned, the enemy found Daniel in prayer and brought the offender before the king. This was not what the king desired. He tried to find a loophole, some way to rescue Daniel from the ferocious jaws of the hungry beasts. But no escape could be found. By the king's order, Daniel was thrown to the lions, while the king spent the night fasting, because his deep concern for Daniel prevented sleep.

> Then, at break of day, the king arose and went in haste to the den of lions. As he came near to the den where Daniel was, he cried out in a tone of anguish. The king declared to Daniel, "O Daniel, servant of the living God, has your God, whom you serve continually, been able to deliver you from the lions?" Then Daniel said to the king, "O king, live forever! My God sent his angel and shut the lions' mouths, and they have not harmed me, because I was found blameless before him; and also before you, O king, I have done no harm." Then the king was exceedingly glad, and commanded that Daniel be taken up out of the den. (Dan. 6:19–23)

Despite the danger of death, Daniel chose prayer and thanksgiving. He valued prayer and his time with Almighty God more than his life. He knew his life without prayer would not be worth living. Willing to give his life for privileged time with God, he prayed openly, boldly, and without shame. Would we do the same?

No Time to Say Thank You

Young children's prayers are dominated by thankfulness. They thank God for every person, animal, toy, and crumb of food. Many moms surely wonder if this lengthy list isn't a stalling tactic to avoid an unwanted broccoli or a clever scheme to delay bedtime. But the widespread phenomenon shows the beauty and the authenticity of these thankful baby prayers.

Unfortunately, as the child grows, the "thank yous" decrease while the "I wants" increase. Often the time is not taken to itemize a thank-you list. This neglect often follows women into adulthood. The "thank you" portion of prayer gets omitted or replaced by a vague thank you tacked at the end. A specific list? Does it really matter? Isn't a general thank you good enough?

God does not need proper etiquette thank yous, but a detailed list acknowledges God's hand in each part of our world: material blessings, family members, friends, and spiritual blessings. When we itemize our thanks in prayer, we perceive blessings clearly and our vision becomes twenty-twenty. We thank God for lightbulbs, prescriptions, a copy of the Bible, a warm bed, for ministering angels, for ambidextrous fingers, for a friend with a penchant for listening, for Jesus, and on and on we return each day and build our gratitude. So let your lists be long and let your thanks flow often.

In the Trenches with Cathy: A few years ago at Thanksgiving, we hosted the family meal at our home. All our guests chipped in to bring tantalizing dishes of food, the usual turkey, southern cornbread stuffing, gravy, and mashed potatoes. In addition, we had all those other good things such as fresh cranberry relish, a crisp garden salad, candied yams, the traditional green bean casserole, and our family favorites—deviled eggs, sweet yellow corn, and yeast rolls. I'm not done reciting our menu because we haven't even walked by the dessert table, laden with pies in flavors of pecan, lemon, pumpkin, cherry, and chocolate.

An hour after the meal, when the adults were cleaning the kitchen and having a cup of coffee to top off very full stomachs, six-year-old grandson Adam strolled into the kitchen. He did what he always does—he opened the refrigerator door and his eyes searched the contents. He stood there long enough for the chilled air to seep across the pine floor to the sink where I stood.

He finally shut the door and said in a voice full of resignation, "Grandma, do you have *anything* to eat in here?" I suspect that many of us relate to Adam's longing. Adam had bypassed a feast that day and thought that my home held nothing tasty within. Because of disappointment in not getting what we want, we may feel that life doesn't hold many good things. Perhaps like Adam, we are holding the door open and longing for something better because all we see are leftovers.

Some refer to life as having mountain moments and valleys, but life is really more like a jogging trail alongside a street; they run parallel to each other, but the speed of cars and runners and what they see are remarkably different. The drivers zoom by and miss the sound of a chirping cardinal or the tree frog suctioned to pine bark. But the walker or runner has a different perspective; she's slowed her pace enough to see a ladybug on a rose or dandelion forcing its stem through a paved path. On a field trip with God, she is refreshed. She may get to say hello to a neighbor, instead of texting her.

Life can be hit and miss. Sunshine and rain fall on the same head, but God can train our inner heart and our outward eyes to see abundance all around us. We can find ten things wrong, or we can find ten things right: longtime married lovers, the downy head of a newborn, orange trumpet flowers, freckles on a tiny nose, an angel-shaped cloud, snowflakes on noses, and girls in white sashes, brown paper packages tied up with strings . . . well, you get the picture. Zoom through life with cloudy eyes focused inward or ask God to allow you to see his bounty with newfound appreciation . . . and give thanks.

Armor of God

Sword: "But thanks be to God, who gives _____ the victory through our Lord Jesus Christ" (1 Cor. 15:57).

Shield: "_____, enter his gates with thanksgiving, and his courts with praise! Give thanks to him; bless his name!" (Ps. 100:4).

Shoes: Therefore, as you, _____, received Christ Jesus the Lord, so walk in him, rooted and built up in him and established in the faith, just as you were taught, abounding in thanksgiving" (Col. 2:6–7).

In the Trenches with Jesus: Of the numerous miracles Jesus performed, physical healing dominates the recordings in the Gospels. Over thirty mentioned individuals received the healing power of the Messiah. However, into one of these healing moments, Jesus brings the question of gratitude. The Gospel of Luke records that Jesus left the area of Galilee and traveled south toward Jerusalem, passing through Samaria, where he came upon a small band of lepers.

Lepers, considered unclean, were cast from society, perhaps never to see family or friends again. They lived among other lepers for protection and companionship, but their lives were hard, burdened by the stigma of a gruesome, disfiguring disease that would eventually lead to a horrid death.

These lepers had heard of Jesus, and from a distance they cried out to him, begging for mercy. They knew he could heal them. He had healed others. This encounter could forever alter their bleak existence and delay their certain death. Heard by the merciful Great Physician, Jesus instructed them to show themselves to the priest. As they walked toward the priest for examination, they were healed. The unthinkable, unimaginable prayer of their hearts answered. They could return home freed from the horror of leprosy!

For most of Jesus's healings the story ends here, but one Samaritan man among the lepers returned to give thanks, and "then Jesus answered, 'Were not ten cleansed? Where are the nine? Was no one found to return and give praise to God except this foreigner?'" (Luke 17:17–18). The Samaritan, not a Jew, grasped the value of thankfulness. This man might not have expected a Jewish rabbi's attention, since the Samaritans had restricted contact with Jews. He knew this truth, that he was considered a dog by the Jews, not even human. From this humbled place of unworthiness, the Samaritan man gave thanks.

What happened to the other nine? Could they have possibly believed they deserved healing or that somehow good health was their right? Jesus brought attention to their absence and the lack of thanksgiving, but he didn't reveal why they failed to express gratitude. We are left with speculation. Why would someone who is given the gift of life after a sentence of death not say thank you to the giver?

Entitlement—The Nemesis of Thankfulness
On July 4, 1776, the Second Continental Congress adopted the United States Declaration of Independence, and a portion reads, "We hold these truths to be self-evident, that all men are created equal, that they are endowed by their Creator with certain

unalienable Rights, that among these are Life, Liberty and the pursuit of Happiness." Unfortunately, some have turned the pursuit of happiness into the right to happiness. Entitlement means "the fact of having a right to something." But as children of God, to what are we really entitled? What does God owe us? What privileges can we demand as a right of birth?

God owes us nothing. Yet, in his infinite goodness, he gives us daily provisions and the greatest gift of his Son. Because of our sin-filled nature, our only true right is death, hell, and separation from God's love. But merciful God has given us so much more. He gives us everything we need for life and godliness. He gives us *everything*! Every good gift comes from above.

God knows our needs, but asking for them defeats a spirit of entitlement. A grateful heart results from asking for bread, God's provision of bread, and eating bread that same day. Ditch the attitude of entitlement. Embrace the truth that our loving God loves to bless us with good gifts, and thanksgiving will flow spontaneously.

My Dog Tag

"I, _____, will give thanks to the LORD with my whole heart; I will recount all of your wonderful deeds" (Ps. 9:1).

In the Trenches with Deanna: I am a fairly thankful person. God's blessings surround me on every side. As I considered this chapter, I wasn't sure what I should share. As I prayed, God brought my attention to something I am rarely thankful for—my body. The conviction stung even as I tried to justify my feelings and attitude.

My body and I do not get along. Thanks to a mild case of cerebral palsy, that seems to become less mild as my age increases, I have limitations and varying degrees of pain. My body doesn't respond as I would like: it doesn't walk, stand, run, or jump well at all. Stairs and rough terrain are obstacles I typically avoid. A wheelchair occasionally gets me where I want to go. My right hand does little to help with anything. My right fingers don't type or move as directed. My list of aches, pains, and general frustrations could fill this chapter.

I honestly believed I simply must endure this body, complaining only when absolutely necessary and doing what I could to treat it well, not making any of the problems worse. But God has used this chapter to unearth a detrimental attitude. I am not just to tolerate the body God has given me—I am called to thankfulness. I'm not quite ready to be thankful for pain or limitations, but I can be thankful for all I can do, which is an incredible amount.

When I was first diagnosed at two, the doctors warned my parents that I would not be as smart as other children and eventually not walk. Before I began college, my mom took me back to see this doctor. She enjoyed telling him of my tennis feats and my class ranking. The doctor was thrilled for us and considered my life a miracle. In his eyes and my mom's I was a *walking* victory story. They were thankful, but from where I unevenly stood, all I could see was how hard my life was. I felt cheated. I wanted a body that worked correctly.

But now I see, I have the body God wants me to have, and it works the way he designed. I might prefer an upgraded model, but I can and will choose to be thankful for all I can do. This is still new to me, and I'm not walking in complete thankfulness, but now that God has my attention, I am confident that with his strength and grace I will *walk* or *roll* in full thanksgiving for this body one day.

If our paths cross, feel free to ask how thankful I am for my body. My prayer . . . that I'll be able to share my victory story with you.

"In," Not "For"

"Thank you," seems the most appropriate *after* prayer when God hears us, moves, and answers positively, but what about those times when we don't see the results we asked for and desperately wanted? What then? How do we follow the Scripture that calls for giving thanks in all things? "Give thanks in all circumstances; for this is the will of God in Christ Jesus for you" (1 Thess. 5:18).

Giving thanks *in* a circumstance is very different than being thankful *for* a circumstance. 1 Thessalonians 5:18 would be hard to embrace if those prepositions were exchanged. We can be *in* a box, but that doesn't mean we are *for* the box. When the situation we find ourselves in is awful, heartbreaking, or just evil, for what can we be thankful? How do we give thanks when too many things seem dismal and out of control? Or after waiting on God, seeking him for specific answers to numerous prayers, and he answers *no* or *wait some more*, how do we then give thanks? After the mess. After the death of a dream. After no change—a prayer of thanksgiving seems not only odd, but also false and empty.

A woman of God can always give thanks for God's faithfulness and love. We can be thankful God will bring victory from what looks like defeat. We don't go to a war zone against evil alone. God, our constant, faithful commanding officer stands beside us in battle and strengthens our weary hands when combat intensifies.

Women warriors of Christ offer thanksgiving for that kind of love and faithfulness even from the trenches of suffering.

Combat Mission for This Week
Thank God throughout your day in all circumstances for his love and faithfulness.

Historical Field Guide

Early Christians recognized the value of prayer and made it part of their daily lives. As the church grew, traditions evolved. One of these was the liturgy of hours. The custom has roots in Judaism. David, in Psalms, tells of praying multiple times a day, and this habit carried on in Daniel's life. The early Christians saw the value of this set-aside time for prayer and created a formal ritual, and village and city church bells rang on the hour as reminders. In the Middle Ages, the very wealthy owned ornate "book of hours" devotionals with Scripture and prayer guides.

While this practice is considered Catholic, praying the seven traditional hours of the day offers training for continual praise. No doubt prayers rise continually from this earth to our Father who is in heaven. Join the throng of those praises and requests. Start a good prayer habit by using this adapted online guide throughout this week.[1] Mark the pages in this book, and lay the book somewhere you frequent throughout the day. Or memorize the short prayers so you can pray them while driving or running errands. The tradition of rich antiquity prayers and steady time with God promises renewal and strength.

Praying the Hours

Lauds (when you wake up)
Glory be to thee, Lord God, Father, Son, and Holy Spirit: as it was in the beginning, is now, and will be forever. Amen.

Prime (when you get out of bed)
A Collect for Grace

Lord God, almighty and everlasting Father, you have brought us in safety to this new day: Preserve us with your mighty power, that we may not fall into sin, nor be overcome by adversity; and in all we do, direct us to the fulfilling of your purpose; through Jesus Christ our Lord. Amen.

Terce (midmorning)
A Collect for Guidance

O heavenly Father, in whom we live and move and have our being: We humbly pray thee so to guide and govern us by thy Holy Spirit, that in all the cares and occupations of our life we may not forget thee, but may remember that we are ever walking in thy sight; through Jesus Christ our Lord. Amen.

Sext (noon)
Blessed Savior, at this hour you hung upon the cross, stretching out your loving arms: Grant that all the peoples of the earth may look to you and be saved; for your tender mercies' sake. Amen.

None (midafternoon)
Savior of the world, by your cross and precious blood
you have redeemed us; Save us and help us, we
humbly beseech you, O Lord.

Vespers (early evening)
O gracious Light,
pure brightness of the everliving Father in heaven,
O Jesus Christ, holy and blessed!
Now as we come to the setting of the sun,
and our eyes behold the vesper light,
we sing thy praises, O God: Father, Son, and Holy Spirit.
Thou art worthy at all times to be praised by happy voices,
O Son of God, O Giver of life,
and to be glorified though all the worlds.

Compline (at bedtime)
A Collect for Aid against Perils

Be our light in the darkness, O Lord, and in your great
mercy defend us from all perils and dangers of this night; for
the love of your only Son, our Savior Jesus Christ. Amen.
Guide us waking, O Lord, and guard us sleeping; that awake
we may watch with Christ, and asleep we may rest in peace.

Matins (when sleep is difficult)
Keep watch, dear Lord, with those who work, or watch, or
weep this night, and give thine angels charge over those who
sleep. Tend the sick, Lord Christ; give rest to the weary, bless
the dying, soothe the suffering, pity the afflicted, shield the
joyous; and all for thy love's sake. Amen.

My Combat Prayer
Dear Lord, create in me a thankful heart.

And be thankful (Col. 3:15).

Tactical Training

1. According to 1 Thessalonians 5:18, giving thanks is a *before*, *during*, and *after* prayer. When do you find it easiest to give thanks? When is it hardest and when do you forget the most often? What will you do to prompt giving thanks in all circumstances?

2. In the encounter with the lepers, why does Jesus draw attention to the lack of gratitude? He doesn't in any other healing. Why this time? What are your thoughts?

3. Entitlement is a huge buzzword today regarding children, teens, and adults. From your childhood, was thanksgiving emphasized or can you see where entitlement may have slipped in? With your children or grandchildren what do you see?

4. The Jewish tradition was to offer thanks before a meal and after a meal. This is not an Old Testament law. Why do you

think the tradition began? What is the value? Do you honor this tradition in your home? Why or why not?

5. Look at the following Scriptures: 1 Chronicles 29:13, Ezra 3:11, Psalm 7:17, Psalm 35:18, and Psalm 69:30. Do you see a pattern? Why do you think praise and thanksgiving go hand in hand?

6. Consider Matthew 26:25–27. Why did Jesus give thanks for this? Why declare it out loud for all to hear?

7. Review your life and give thanks for something you were not thankful for at the time. What was the circumstance? Why are you thankful now? If you were able to think of something, can you see how this supports 1 Thessalonians 5:18?

8. Who do you know that has a thankful heart? What other qualities does that person have? How did that person develop a grateful spirit? What plan can you make to boost your gratitude?

My Diary from the Trenches

Expect our Father to increase spontaneous thanksgiving. Record your victories.

Chapter Twelve

Praise After Good News

Miriam and Mary

"Great is the LORD, and greatly to be praised, and his greatness is unsearchable." —Psalm 145:3

Both recruits and seasoned soldiers—and every rank in between—are the Lord's winning women. As we taught and wrote together, we enjoyed presenting and writing from the perspective of the older woman and the younger woman, and we have experienced the blessings of filling the generation gap in time spent together. Deanna's contagious joy and Bible knowledge blessed Cathy, and Deanna gleaned from Cathy's contentment and longtime experience of mentoring women. We urge any woman to get to know people younger and older than you. Pray about those connections and ask our Father to lead you to other winning women because within those relationships are mutual and intended blessings. This last chapter covers the praise of the young woman, Mary, and Deanna writes that portion, while Cathy writes about Miriam.

Unplanned Pregnancy and Praise—
Matthew 1:18–25; Luke 1:26–56

Mary, probably in her early teens, received startling news. The announcement would forever change her life, and that news of a Messiah would continue to change lives. Gabriel, an angel sent from God, brought glad tidings to a young unwed girl. Christmas carols tell the story thousands of years later. How exciting to be Mary! Mother of the Son of God! But in the joyous news of the impending arrival of the King of Kings, don't forget this girl has to tell her parents and fiancé that she is pregnant by the Holy Spirit.

Maybe Mary has never told a lie, not even one. Maybe honesty characterizes the highly favored, chosen of God. Even then the news would be hard to tell Joseph, her fiancé, who will not believe her extraordinary story and plan to quietly divorce her when he receives the "glad tidings of great joy." To him, surely his doubts sting and his suspicions rage, but God allows this part of the story, too. God could have alerted Joseph, her family, and her friends to make the initial announcement easier for the young, unwed, pregnant teenager, but God doesn't. Mary, certain of God's favor and blessing, must endure any scoffing of the judgmental or disdain of the self-righteous.

Mary leaves town to visit Zechariah and Elizabeth, maybe to escape gossip or to enjoy the miracles of God with her elderly cousins. This elderly couple, unexpectedly pregnant, will have the honor of being the parents of John the Baptist, the forerunner for Christ. When young Mary arrives at her cousins' home, the unborn baby in Elizabeth's womb jumps for joy and recognizes the Savior, unborn in Mary's womb. The first person to recognize the Christ is an unborn child. Incredible! Surely this sensational welcome refreshes and thrills young Mary. The older

Elizabeth's warmth and wisdom embrace her as the mother of Jesus Christ, the Messiah, and Savior of the world.

I, the younger writer of this book, remember so vividly the thrill of being an expectant mommy! I didn't just float on clouds; I soared and somersaulted through the skies of joy and delight. Mary probably experienced exhilarating emotions, too. Even though she would have rough days ahead—the suspicions of family and friends, backaches, swollen ankles, donkey rides, unglamorous delivery, no epidural—Mary had many reasons for praising her Heavenly Father—that first flutter in her womb and later holding in her arms the Prince of Peace. Mary recognized the awesomeness of the God of Creation!

> And Mary said, "My soul magnifies the Lord, and my spirit rejoices in God my Savior, for he has looked on the humble estate of his servant. For behold, from now on all generations will call me blessed; for he who is mighty has done great things for me, and holy is his name. And his mercy is for those who fear him from generation to generation. He has shown strength with his arm; he has scattered the proud in the thoughts of their hearts; he has brought down the mighty from their thrones and exalted those of humble estate; he has filled the hungry with good things, and the rich he has sent away empty. He has helped his servant Israel, in remembrance of his mercy, as he spoke to our fathers, to Abraham and to his offspring forever." (Luke 1:46–55)

In the presence of the older Elizabeth, young Mary found her song of *after* praise for an incredible story that was about to unfold for all the earth.

In the Trenches with Jesus: As Jesus enters the city from the Mount of Olives on the back of a colt, the crowd spreads their cloaks and palm branches on the ground in front of him. They voice praise: "Blessed is the King who comes in the name of the Lord! Peace in heaven and glory in the highest!" (Luke 19:38).

Some of the religious leaders take offense at this display of praise and worship and demand that Jesus stop his followers. But Jesus, who knows the value of praise, refuses. "I tell you, if these were silent, the very stones would cry out" (Luke 19:40). Jesus receives praise because his incredible greatness demands it. If not our praise—then the rocks will declare his splendor. Praise draws us to our Creator. When the realization of the grandeur of the Almighty God settles into hearts and minds, praise results and should not be silenced but fully embraced and joyfully exclaimed. Let your voice cry out with the crowd from Jerusalem, "Hosanna to the Son of David! Blessed is he who comes in the name of the Lord! Hosanna in the highest!" (Matt. 21:9).

Armor of God

Sword: "Shout for joy to God, _____; sing the glory of his name; give to him glorious praise!" (Ps. 66:1–2).

Shield: "_____, Praise the LORD! Praise God in his sanctuary; praise him in his mighty heavens! Praise him for his mighty deeds; praise him according to his excellent greatness! Let everything that has breath praise the LORD! _____, Praise the LORD!" (Ps. 150:1–2, 6).

Shoes: "I, _____, will bless the LORD at all times; his praise shall continually be in my mouth" (Ps. 34:1).

In the Trenches with Deanna: I am a member of a singing family. Not a glamorous band or music group, we are pickup truck singers. We sing along to the radio at its and our full volume. We love singing, but I must confess my favorite sing-alongs are on road trips. Watching my family praise God together as we travel down highways does my heart good. I can vividly picture my son—eyes closed and hand lifted—worshiping the Shepherd of his soul with all his being. And my daughter, her sweet voice lifted with her head thrown back, as she praises her Maker and Redeemer. Finally, my cowboy, one hand on the wheel and one hand tapping the wheel as he joins his children's joyful impromptu worship service. As I sit in the passenger seat of that huge Dodge Ram truck, I have no choice but to join them. My soul cries out, and like the crowd thousands of years before— I too must worship; no rock will take my place in our time of highway praise.

The Blessings of Praise

Throughout Scripture we are charged with praising God for his holiness, mighty deeds, wondrous works, and more. However, God doesn't need our praise, for he is complete and secure without. So why does he command our worship? Praise pours forth in response to the wholeness of God, but it also offers hidden blessings for those who worship daily.

Choosing to praise God regardless of circumstances changes a woman's focus and perspective. Eyes, once entranced by the world's lures or troubles, shift and rediscover the might and power of God. Praise credits and honors the one most deserving. Continual praise results in a humble and softened heart. Finally, praise brings the participant into the presence of God, right into his courts (Ps. 100), and in his presence there is joy (Ps. 21:6). Ultimately praise changes us. While we praise our Lord and Master, he does what only he can do in the soil of our hearts—he plants in us the image of Jesus.

Dog Tag Scripture

"_____, sing to him, sing praises to him; tell of all his wondrous works!" (1 Chron. 16:9).

> Until God opens the next door for you, praise him in the hallway. —2 Fish Restaurant[1]
>
> "I praise you, for I am fearfully and wonderfully made. Wonderful are your works; my soul knows it very well. —Psalm 139:14

Miriam—a Leader Full of Praise

We read this sentence that reminds us of Miriam: Only God can turn a mess into a message, a test into a testimony, a trial into triumph, and a victim into a victory. If our ancient sister Miriam read that after her rescue from slavery, I imagine her wrinkled face would break out in a huge grin, and she'd say "Amen!" Miriam was a woman like us, a mixture of failings and successes, who would ultimately be delivered by the hand of God. In Micah 6:4, God declares that he had chosen a group of siblings to lead Israel: Miriam, Aaron, and Moses (in birth order). Miriam's leadership and quick thinking showed up at an early age when she watched over her brother Moses. At one time, she criticized Moses's choices and God rebuked her. Called a prophetess, she led the women in a praise song and dancing at the Sea of Reeds in a celebration of God's goodness.

By the time the merriment takes place at the Sea of Reeds, Miriam is in her late eighties to mid-nineties. Imagine a respected but sprightly senior woman, who takes up a timbrel, hikes up her robe—just a bit—and in true rejoicing she leads the women to sing and dance a praise chorus. "Sing to the LORD, for he is highly exalted. Both horse and driver he has hurled into the sea" (Exod. 15:21 NIV). Terri Guillemet's sentiment defines such moments: "It is of course possible to dance a prayer."

Dearest older women, I, Cathy, earnestly ask that you set the example of praise for younger women. And if you have a root of bitterness, ask the Master Gardener to dig it out, replant a new nature, and nourish you with living water. Every time I read Miriam's story, I'm excited about the years ahead, and I wonder how God will continue my service to him because Miriam lived another forty years as a prophetess for Israel.

In the Trenches with Cathy: Sometimes God goes bump in the night. A friend, Julie, called to praise God and share this story with me. She had had a particularly difficult day with her aging mother. Julie had arranged a day full of pampering for her mom, who suffers from various ailments. For every positive thing that happened that day, her mother found three things about which to complain. If you've ever spent a day with a heavy complainer, you know what happens—whininess is contagious. Soon Julie grumbled in her spirit, and exhaustion and frustration nagged at her because her mother's cantankerous attitude had tainted the well-planned day.

At Julie's bedtime, after tossing and turning, sleep had not arrived but a headache had. She got up to get Tylenol from the same cabinet where she kept her nightly reading material and a few books she had finished. When she reached for the pills, my book *A Still and Quiet Soul—Embracing Contentment* thumped down onto the counter. She said, "Even the title blessed me in that split second," reminding her of God's provision and presence. She casually flipped open the pages and they separated to the third chapter: "Spirit Wilt—Complaining Sabotages Contentment," and the theme Scripture: "Do all things without grumbling" (Phil. 2:14).

Immediately, Julie was overwhelmed by the goodness of God to define her day so vividly, and to walk her beside still waters. He steered her toward the peace and calm of God instead of the discontents of the day. She praised God that night, and the next morning she wrote a thank-you note to me. Praise changed her, turned her thoughts around, and allowed the sweet Holy Spirit to spritz her with living water. That night, her mind relaxed, she slept, and the morning brought the freshness and hydration needed for that day.

Be ready to give praise to God often, for he helps you every minute of every hour. Yes, sometimes God really goes bump in the night.

Create a Template of Praise When You Are Young

By the time a woman matures in years, she has chosen paths and attitudes that shaped the song that drifts out from her life. Each time she allowed God's Spirit to guide, she took in his offer of holiness. If she chose to give in to the influence of the devil, she took on his contrary nature. From the springy curls of youth to gray hair, we make choices to praise God or join the crankiness of the world. From those choices and influences, we present a song to the world—soothing joy or the disharmony of bitterness.

Scripture presents several portraits of the aged. God says that those who have decades of years accumulated, who are rooted in him, will thrive much like a green tree planted by a stream that produces fruit in each season, even in the vintage years (Ps. 1:3; Jer. 17:8). In later life, Solomon took missteps on an opposing path that led him away from God and invited misery into his life. His foreign wives "turned his heart after other gods, and his heart was not fully devoted to the LORD his God" (1 Kings 11:4 NIV). Or some have set a heart pattern of complaining when younger, noticing wrongs, and becoming blind to blessings that surrounded them every second. Their unpleasant attitude crowded out holiness.

At least one other possibility exists to explain why a woman who has been kind and loving all her life might become a whiner in her last years. Our aged, shrinking, and sometimes diseased brains deteriorate and become senile, and then we may no longer have the ability to make the best choices, such as yielding to the Holy Spirit. Some of you are a caregiver for an older Christian who has had a distinct personality change, and you are hurt to see a person of praise become ill-tempered, foul-mouthed, and accusing in their old age. Be aware . . . their mind may no longer be functional enough to yield to God's holy urgings. Caregiving, and not having adequate time for personal grooming or house-hold needs, can be a real test of faith. I fully believe my brother James's way is the high road for those of us called to be care-givers for many years: "Count it all joy, my [sisters], when you meet trials of various kinds," because "you know that the testing of your faith produces steadfastness. And let steadfastness have its full effect, that you may be perfect and complete, lacking in nothing" (James 1:2–5).

When the word "mystery" appears in the Bible, I'm intrigued because I have come across something larger than me, something beyond my comprehension at the hem of the majestic robe of God. God works in mysterious ways and he remains beyond my understanding. My life and your life are mysterious. We exist because God ordained our existence, and we continue in life because God decrees each breath. Allow God entrance into your heart. Give him the key. Don't make him wait outside on the stoop, knocking and longing to enter.

I encourage you to build a template of praise as you mature. Make a habit of praise. Your joyful adoration will allow those around you to hear a sweet song about Jesus, your audience of one. So with every breath ...

... Let there be praise . . . let there be praise . . . let there be praise.

Combat Mission for This Week
Praise God in private and in public.

Historical Field Guide

Current prayer ministries have adapted a Jewish custom to make quilted or knitted prayer shawls. As they assemble these shawls, they pray over the one who eventually receives the covering, and a note of explanation accompanies the shawl upon presentation. While no power exists within the cloth, the requests made during the creation of the shawl reach God, who has infinite power and mercy toward sufferers.

The Jewish prayer shawl, *tallit* (meaning "little tent"), evolved from an outer garment men wore during the Mosaic period that had tassels at the corners, including a blue thread (signifying nobility, Num. 15:37–41). To get an accurate picture of the prayer shawl garment, imagine a flat, seamless rectangle, fringed at the corners, with a hole in the middle to pull over the head.

The prayer covering was the last garment put on each day, a visual reminder that Israel was set apart from the world, a nation of priests. The fringe at the corners was made of a mixture of linen and wool, but Deuteronomy 22:11 forbade the mixture of linen and wool in their everyday clothing. Current traditional Jewish prayer shawls contain multiple strings tied into systematic knots that make fringes (*tzitzit*). The knots represent the number of laws given to Israel.[2]

Prayer shawls come in different shapes, colors, and fringes, but all lead back to closeting one's self in the small tent, symbolic of separating oneself from the world. In that blessed place one can worship, praise, and seek God's blessing. One Jewish tradition explains that the square of the cloth represents all of God, while the fringe represents the small portion of God that he has allowed us to glimpse and understand.[3]

Under the old law, only the men were required to wear this garment. Some even think it's possible that the seamless garment of Christ that was gambled for at the foot of the cross was a prayer garment. Also, when Jesus mentioned going into a closet to commune with God, he may have had the prayer shawl, the little tent, in mind. Sequestering one's self by whatever means to be alone with God will always equal blessings.

My Combat Prayer
Father, anoint me with the oil of joy and praise.

You (Jesus) have loved righteousness and hated wickedness; therefore God, your God, has anointed you with the oil of gladness beyond your companions (Heb. 1:9).

Tactical Training

1. Can you imagine yourself in Mary's sandals? How would you have responded? What reaction would you have had if you were Mary's mom or friend? Does the thought of praise cross your mind? Why or why not?

2. Praise is our response to the majesty of God. What are some of your favorite praise songs? Why are they your favorites? Listen this week to some new songs of praise and add a few to your praise playlist or add a few old hymns. Mix up your time of worship; keep it fresh and alive.

3. Praise and worship are often used interchangeably or together. Look at Psalm 66:4. What is the difference? Consider Romans 12:1 as you think through your answer. What do you spend more time doing: praise or worship? Consider ways to increase both—think out of the box.

4. Schedule some private praise time this week. Just you and God. Be willing to let the Spirit direct and free you to enjoy your time in God's presence. Psalm 150 is a great place to start.

5. Read Micah 6:4 and Exodus 15:20. What plan and purpose for Miriam are mentioned in these verses?

6. Read these Scriptures for a timeline of Miriam's life and note the milestones mentioned: Numbers 26:59; Exodus 2:1–10; 15:1, 19–21; Numbers 12; Numbers 20:1. What did you learn about Miriam?

7. Miriam was an aged woman by the time she took up the tambourine and led the women in praise. How do you envision your aging? Read Isaiah 46:3–5. God promised to be with Israel, carrying them even when their hair grew gray. Do you know an aged person of praise? How did a spirit of praise develop?

8. Read Psalm 92:12–15. What praise does the songwriter say will be on the lips of the righteous at old age? Practice praise, now and always, to allow God to create a template of joy in your spirit.

My Diary from the Trenches

Verbally praise God five times each day this week. Record your
victories.

Notes

Chapter 1

[1] Joseph S. Exell and Henry Donald Maurice Spence-Jones, "Commentary on 1 Samuel 12:17," *The Pulpit Commentaries*, www.studylight.org/commentaries /tpc/1-samuel-12.html.1897.

[2] Richard J. Foster, *Celebration of Discipline: The Path to Spiritual Growth*. 1990 ed. San Francisco: Harper & Row, 1978. 45.

[3] Hymn Stories: "A Mighty Fortress Is Our God," Tim Challies - http:// www.challies.com/articles/hymn-stories-a-mighty-fortress-is-our-god.

Chapter 2

[1] "Intercede," Online Etymology Dictionary, accessed August 17, 2015, http://www.etymonline.com/index.php?term=intercede.

[2] Used by permission.

[3] Bergh, F.T. (1909), "Genuflexion, in "The Catholic Encyclopedia." (New York: Robert Appleton Company), accessed December 31, 2016 from New Advent: http://www.newadvent.org/cathen/06423a.htm.

[4] John Coke Fowler, Esq, "Church Pews, Their Origin and Legal Incidents, with Some Observations on the Propriety of Abolishing Them, in Three Chapters" (London: Francis & John Rivington, 1844), accessed December 31, 2016, http://anglicanhistory.org/misc/freechurch/fowler_pews1844.html.

[5] Ronald Dunn, "Don't Just Stand There, Pray Something: The Incredible Power of Intercessory Prayer" (Nashville: T. Nelson, 1992).

Chapter 3

[1] "Yom Kippur," Judaism 101 (website), accessed October 15, 2016, http:// www.jewfaq.org/holiday4.htm#YKL.

Chapter 4

[1] "A Christian Heritage," Joseph Smith (website linked to website of the Church of Jesus Christ of Latter-day Saints), September 11, 2013, https:// josephsmith.net/article/a-christian-heritage?lang=eng.

Chapter 5

[1] Doug Goins, "The Preparation of Zechariah and Elizabeth," sermon given to Peninsula Bible Church, November 17, 1985, Discovery Publishing, http://www.pbc.org/system/message_files/6168/3896.html.

[2] Matthew Henry, "Luke 1:10," *Concise Commentary on the Whole Bible,* BibleHub, accessed September 15, 2015, http://biblehub.com/luke/1-10.htm.

[3] "Orans Gesture (Orant Posture)," Symboldictionary.net, accessed August 8, 2015, http://symboldictionary.net/?p=2271.

Chapter 6

[1] Katherine Russell, "15 Famous Quotes and 5 Principles About Prayer," *Christian Post,* accessed June 13, 2016, http://ipost.christianpost.com/post/15-famous-quotes-and-5-principles-about-prayer.

[2] Oswald Chambers, accessed January 2, 2017, https://www.goodreads.com/author/quotes/41469.Oswald_Chambers.

[3] Mark Herringshaw, "John Wesley's *Covenant Prayer,*" *Prayer, Plain and Simple* (blog), Beliefnet.com, accessed October 7, 2015, http://www.beliefnet.com/columnists/prayerplainandsimple/2010/02/john-wesleys-covenant-prayer-1.html#q8824tYiTLCMjOuS.99.

Chapter 7

[1] Max Lucado, Twitter post, July 27, 2016, 12:01 P.M., http://twitter.com/maxlucado.

[2] John Foxe, *Foxe's Book of Martyrs* (Lexington, KY: John C. Winston Co., 2015), 7.

Chapter 8

[1] Latayne C. Scott, *The Hinge of Your History: The Phases of Faith* (North Charleston, SC: CreateSpace Publishing, 2010).

[2] Matthew Henry, *Matthew Henry Commentary in One Volume* (Grand Rapids: Zondervon, 1961), 32.

[3] *Anne of Green Gables,* directed by Kevin Sullivan and Trudy Grant, performed by Megan Follows, Colleen Dewhurst, Richard Farnsworth (Canada: Sullivan Entertainment, 1985), DVD.

[4] Betsy Williams, *Breath Prayers for Women: Simple Whispers That Keep You in God's Presence* (Colorado Springs: Honor Books, 2004).

[5] Robert Munce, *Grace Livingston Hill* (Wheaton, IL: Tyndale House, 1986).

Chapter 9

[1] Charles H. Spurgeon, *The Pastor in Prayer: Being a Choice Selection of C. H. Spurgeon's Sunday Morning Prayers* (Pasedena, TX: Pilgrim Publications, 1971), foreward.

Chapter 10

[1] Eugene Peterson, "Sin: David and Bathsheba," *Leap Over a Wall: Earthy Spirituality for Everyday Christians* (New York: HarperCollins, 1998), 181–82.

[2] Oswald Chambers, quote posted January 18, 2016, utmost.org, http://utmost.org/quotes/2262/.

[3] Latayne C. Scott, *Passion, Power, Proxy, Release: Scriptures, Poems, and Devotional Thoughts for Communion and Worship Services* (Albuquerque: Trinity Southwest University Press, 2016), 30.

[4] Albert Barnes, *Barnes' Notes on the Bible*, "Amos 1:3," BibleHub, accessed July 15, 2016, http://biblehub.com/commentaries/amos/1-3.htm.

[5] Herbert V. Prochnow and Herbert V. Prochnow Jr., *The Toastmaster's Treasure Chest* (San Fransisco: Harper & Row, 1979), 248, entry 2256.

[6] Robert Young, "Bathsheba," *Young's Analytical Concordance to the Bible*, 22nd ed. (Grand Rapids: Wm. B. Eerdmans, 1969), 72.

[7] Roy Ratcliff and Lindy Adams, *Dark Journey, Deep Grace: Jeffrey Dahmer's Story of Faith* (Abilene, TX: Leafwood Publishers, 2006).

Chapter 11

[1] "Praying the Psalms," accessed October 2016, http://palm.philippians-1-20.us/hours.htm.

Chapter 12

[1] Lois Tverberg, "What's So Wrong with Mixing Wool & Linen?" *Our Rabbi Jesus* (blog), July 2, 2013, http://ourrabbijesus.com/articles/whats-so-wrong-with-mixing-wool-linen/.

[2] Jim Barbarossa, "Facts, Traditions and History About Prayer Shawl, Tallit, Tallits, and Prayer Shawls," The Shofar Man (website), accessed August 21, 2016, http://theshofarman.com/tallit-prayershawlfactsandhistory.htm.

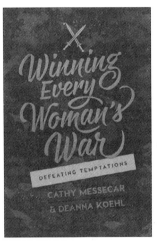

Praise for

Winning Women Pray

"Simple. Practical. Challenging. Reading *Winning Women Pray* helped me tap into the power of communicating with God."

—**Lynne Gentry,** author of The Carthage Chronicles series (Howard Books)

"AWESOME! I loved the book! Chapter One had me whipping out my highlighter. Each 'Tactical Training' section made me dig deep. And personalizing the 'Armor of God' Scriptures by actually writing in my name was powerful. I applaud the authors for their transparency about their struggles, showing they are real women not much different than me. Finally, the book caused me to completely examine my prayer life and gave me a good shaking up. I gained lessons I won't soon forget."

—**Ethel Oliver,** Preacher's wife, women's Bible study leader, and career student of the Bible

"I am a big believer in the power of prayer and how it can change my relationship with God. This book changed how I see my prayers and how God wants me to use my prayer life. He wants a relationship before, during, and after! He wants me to sit down, pray, and have a conversation over coffee, just as I would with my best friend. Only then will I really begin to understand how he wants me to pray. Prayer is our gift from our heavenly Father—let us learn to love and use that gift with wisdom."

—**Stacey Faulkner,** wife, mother of 3, yoga teacher, health coach

"A heart-felt, wise, grace-filled, and touching book—*Winning Women Pray* uses truth from God's Word to encourage prayer before, during, and after life events by including both well-known and not-so-well-known stories from the Bible as examples. The 'In the Trenches' sections offer reminiscent accounts from both authors that may make you chuckle or tear up a little as you read about their intimate moments with God."

—**Tanya Scheler,** wife, mother, child of God

"Prayer in the life of a Christian is a life-link to the Father; but like the disciples of Jesus, we often do not know how to pray. *Winning Women Pray* blends personal experiences with stories from Scripture about prayer, giving the reader some meat to digest while working through the thought questions at the end of each chapter. While it would be an excellent study to teach someone about prayer, it also is a refreshing study for those of us more mature in the faith and a reminder of how important prayer is in our walk with God."

> —**Deanna Brooks,** first female Bible major at Harding, ladies' class teacher, and retreat speaker

"Plug into God's power not just daily but continually. The power of prayer had never occurred to me before in the way it's presented. I have been truly blessed by reading this book and look forward to spending many more hours in studying it. I hope this book will bless the lives of many more women. Plug into the power of God by prayer."

> —**Linda Reeve,** retired teacher, wife, mother, and Bible student

"*Winning Women Pray* is thoughtfully written and organized for personal or group studies. The personal antidotes are engaging and the questions made me search my heart. I highly recommend *Winning Women Pray* for its unique and well-organized walk through the lives of some of the Bible's greatest men and women."

> —**Sherrie Hansen,** author of *Love Notes*

"I would highly recommend the book *Winning Women Pray*. It is well written and would be a wonderful study for a ladies' class. I most enjoyed the 'In The Trenches' stories by Cathy and Deanna. Also, the 'My Dog Tag' section in each of the lessons makes the study become more personal, seeing my name in the Scriptures. The 'My Diary from the Trenches' section helped me to work out my understanding of the lesson and the application in my life. Overall, I know my prayer life will increase and be of more value to me having studied this book."

> —**Debbie Hendrix,** preschool and ladies' Bible class teacher, administrator of the Facebook group, Women of the Churches of Christ

"*Winning Women Pray* is an easy-to-read book. Cathy and Deanna use examples of before, during, and after prayers to emphasize that prayer is a powerful tool which helps us fight Satan's wiles and also helps draw us closer to God. They use not only the example of Jesus's prayer life, but other prayers from the Bible and times of prayer from their personal lives together to encourage women to engage in a more vibrant prayer life. It is a great encouragement to both the novice who realizes her need for a stronger prayer life and is an equal encouragement for the woman who has prayed for years."

—**Carrie Blunt,** wife, mother, member Western Hills Church of Christ

"*Winning Women Pray* touched home on so many things in my current prayer life. The questions I've had were answered in this book. I also had things brought to light that I've never considered before. *Winning Women Pray* is a book for all women and something I will definitely reread over and over again. I will be purchasing copies for both of my ladies bible classes at church and for my prison ministry. This is one book I will always recommend."

—**Kris Burton,** the farmer's wife

"This book not only shows a great depth of scriptural knowledge that's often lacking in many 'women's books,' but also calls on a rich heritage of faith. The vulnerability and transparency of failures and triumphs depicted in the authors' lives, too, is refreshing and inspiring."

—**Latayne C. Scott,** author of *The Hinge of Your History*; *Passion, Power, Proxy, Release*; *The Mormon Mirage*; and others

"*Winning Women Pray* is a delightful journey into the workings of prayer and how to apply them to one's life in effectual and personal ways. Each chapter highlights aspects of prayer and invites the reader to engage with wholehearted passion and enthusiasm. The 'Tactical Training,' 'Combat Prayers,' and 'Diary' are a wonderful way to guide women into a deeper connection with Christ. I salute Messecar and Koehl for providing this much-needed resource for today's busy woman. So highly recommended!"

—**Sharlene MacLaren,** Award-Winning author of 18 faith-based novels, including *Summer on Sunset Ridge*; book one in the Forever Freedom series